TECHNICAL
REPORT

Evaluation of the Patient Safety Improvement Corps

Experiences of the First Two Groups of Trainees

Stephanie S. Teleki, Cheryl L. Damberg,
Melony E. Sorbero, Allen Fremont,
Lily Bradley, Donna O. Farley

Sponsored by the Agency for Healthcare Research and Quality

RAND HEALTH

The research described in this report was carried out in RAND Health, a division of the RAND Corporation. This work was sponsored by the Agency for Healthcare Research and Quality.

Library of Congress Cataloging-in-Publication Data

Evaluation of the Patient Safety Improvement Corps : experiences of the first two groups of trainees / Stephanie S. Teleki ... [et al.].
      p. cm.
   "TR-407."
   ISBN-13: 978-0-8330-3992-7 (pbk. : alk. paper)
   1. Hospitals—Safety measures. 2. Medical errors—Prevention. 3. Medical care—Quality control.
I. Teleki, Stephanie. II. Rand Corporation.
   [DNLM: 1. Patient Safety Improvement Corps (U.S.) 2. Education, Continuing—United States. 3. Health Occupations—education—United States. 4. Government Programs—United States. 5. Medical Errors— prevention & control—United States. 6. Safety Management—United States. W 18 E8965 2006]

RA969.9.E93 2006
362.1068'4—dc22

                                                                                    2006021712

The RAND Corporation is a nonprofit research organization providing objective analysis and effective solutions that address the challenges facing the public and private sectors around the world. RAND's publications do not necessarily reflect the opinions of its research clients and sponsors.

RAND® is a registered trademark.

A profile of RAND Health, abstracts of its publications, and ordering information can be found on the RAND Health home page at www.rand.org/health.

Published 2006 by the RAND Corporation
1776 Main Street, P.O. Box 2138, Santa Monica, CA 90407-2138
1200 South Hayes Street, Arlington, VA 22202-5050
4570 Fifth Avenue, Suite 600, Pittsburgh, PA 15213
RAND URL: http://www.rand.org/
To order RAND documents or to obtain additional information, contact
Distribution Services: Telephone: (310) 451-7002;
Fax: (310) 451-6915; Email: order@rand.org

Preface

Since 2000, the Agency for Healthcare Research and Quality (AHRQ) has had a congressional mandate to take a leadership role in helping health care providers reduce medical errors and improve patient safety. As part of its patient safety initiative, AHRQ established the Patient Safety Improvement Corps (PSIC) in partnership with the Department of Veterans Affairs (VA) National Center for Patient Safety (NCPS), which is known for its patient safety expertise. The goal of the PSIC is to improve patient safety across the nation by training health care professionals in core patient safety knowledge, skills, and tools. The core content of the curriculum was developed by AHRQ based upon the findings of a feasibility study as well as consultation with experts and key stakeholders. Through an interagency agreement, AHRQ contracted with the VA NCPS to conduct the training.

In September 2002, AHRQ contracted with the RAND Corporation to serve as the Patient Safety Evaluation Center. Under a four-year contract, the evaluation center is responsible for performing a longitudinal, formative evaluation of the full scope of AHRQ's patient safety activities and for providing regular feedback to support the continuing improvement of the initiative over the evaluation period. In its evaluation, RAND has tracked the patient safety research funded by AHRQ, assessed AHRQ's activities to translate that research into action, and evaluated the impact of these efforts. Each year, RAND has produced an annual evaluation report that provides an update on the evolution and current status of the priorities and activities being undertaken as part of the AHRQ patient safety initiative. Additionally, RAND has produced separate, in-depth reports on specific evaluation topics.

This document is one such stand-alone report. Given the central role of the PSIC in the AHRQ patient safety initiative, a focused assessment of the PSIC has been an important part of the overall patient safety evaluation. This report presents the initial results of RAND's evaluation of the PSIC. Perceptions and experiences are documented for the first two groups of trainees who have completed the PSIC training. For the first group, information was gathered at the end of their training in May 2004, as well as one year later, after they had time to apply what they had learned. For the second group, information was gathered at the end of their training in May 2005. Updated PSIC evaluation results that draw upon data collected in 2006 will be presented in RAND's fourth annual evaluation report.

This report is intended primarily for use by AHRQ and the VA, to help inform future programming decisions. It also will be of interest to national and state policymakers, health care organizations and clinical practitioners, patient-advocacy organizations, health researchers, and others with responsibilities for ensuring that patients are not harmed by the health care they receive.

This work was sponsored by the Agency for Healthcare Research and Quality under Contract No. 290-02-0010, for which James B. Battles serves as project officer. The research was conducted in RAND Health, a division of the RAND Corporation. A profile of RAND Health, abstracts of its publications, and ordering information can be found at www.rand.org/health.

Contents

Figures

Tables

Glossary

Adverse Event: An injury caused by medical management rather than the underlying disease or condition of the patient (IOM, 2000).

Close Call: An event or situation that did not produce patient injury, but only because of chance. This good fortune might reflect robustness of the patient (e.g., a patient with a penicillin allergy receives penicillin, but has no reaction) or a fortuitous, timely intervention (e.g., a nurse happens to realize that a physician wrote an order in the wrong chart). Such events have also been termed "near miss" incidents (AHRQ Patient Safety Network Glossary, 2006).

High-alert medications: Drugs that bear a heightened risk of causing significant patient harm when they are used in error (Institute for Safe Medication Practices, 2006).

High-Reliability Organizations (HROs): Organizations that operate under very trying conditions all the time yet manage to have fewer than their fair share of accidents are referred to collectively as high-reliability organizations; examples include power grid dispatching centers, air traffic control systems, nuclear aircraft carriers, nuclear power generating plants, and hospital emergency departments (Weick and Sutcliffe, 2001). HROs focus on mindfulness, which has several hallmarks including

- Preoccupation with failure: HROs treat any lapse as a symptom that something is wrong with the system, encourage reporting of errors, and use near-miss experiences for what can be learned. They are wary of the potential liabilities of success including complacency, the temptation to reduce margins of safety, and the drift into automatic processing (Weick and Sutcliffe, 2001).
- Commitment to resilience: HROs develop capacities to detect unexpected threats and contain them before they cause harm, or bounce back when they do (Weick and Sutcliffe, 2001).
- Sensitivity to operations: HROs are attentive to issues at the frontline where real work gets done and have a well-developed situational awareness that enables them to make continuous adjustments that prevent errors from accumulating and enlarging. That is, they notice anomalies while they are still tractable and can be isolated (Weick and Sutcliffe, 2001).
- Deference to expertise: HROs attempt to avoid rigid hierarchies and their inherent vulnerabilities by pushing decisionmaking "down and around." This is not to be misconstrued as down to the person with the most experience, but rather pushing the decisionmaking down to the front line (i.e., migrating it to the people with the most expertise) (Weick and Sutcliffe, 2001).
- Reluctance to accept simplification: HROs take deliberate steps to create more complete and nuanced pictures (Weick and Sutcliffe, 2001).
- Culture: HROs have a culture of shared values (what is important) and beliefs (how things work) that interact with an organization's or group's structure(s) and control system(s) to produce behavioral norms (the way we do things) (Reason, 1997).
- Culture of safety: HROs have a commitment to safety that permeates all levels of their organization, from front-line personnel to executive management (AHRQ Patient Safety Network Glossary, 2006).

Healthcare Failure Mode and Effects Analysis (HFMEA): A process used to proactively evaluate system vulnerabilities before a close call occurs. This process has been used by the engineering community for many years. HFMEA is a hybrid technique that was developed by the VA National Center for Patient Safety; it draws upon the methods used in FMEA and applies them to the health care field (DeRosier et al., 2002).

Just Culture: A culture that recognizes that competent professionals make mistakes and acknowledges that even competent professionals will develop unhealthy norms (e.g., shortcuts, "routine rule violations"), but has zero tolerance for reckless behavior (i.e., conscious disregard of a visible, significant risk) (AHRQ Patient Safety Network Glossary, 2006).

Mandatory Reporting System: A required reporting system that usually focuses on specific cases that involve serious harm or death, may result in fines or penalties relative to the specific case, and information about the event may become known to the public. Such systems ensure a response to specific reports of serious injury, hold organizations and providers accountable for maintaining safety, respond to the public's right to know, and provide incentives to health care organizations to implement internal safety systems that reduce the likelihood of such events occurring (IOM, 2002).

Medical Error: The failure of a planned action to be completed as intended (i.e., error of execution) or the use of a wrong plan to achieve an aim (i.e., error of planning) (IOM, 2002).

Near Miss: An event or situation that did not produce patient injury, but only because of chance. This good fortune might reflect robustness of the patient (e.g., a patient with a penicillin allergy receives penicillin, but has no reaction) or a fortuitous, timely intervention (e.g., a nurse happens to realize that a physician wrote an order in the wrong chart). A near miss is synonymous with a close call (AHRQ Patient Safety Network Glossary, 2006).

Never Event: Events that are (1) clearly identifiable and measurable, and therefore feasible to include in a reporting system; (2) of a nature such that the risk of occurrence is significantly influenced by the policies and procedures of the health care facility; and (3) of concern to both health care providers and the public. To qualify for this core list of serious reportable events, an event had to be unambiguous, usually preventable, serious, and one or more of the following: (1) adverse' (2) indicative of a problem in a health care facility's safety systems' and/or (3) important for public credibility or public accountability (Kizer, 2005).

Patient Safety: Freedom from accidental injury (IOM, 2000).

Patient Safety Officer: A person who manages patient safety activities (e.g., Root Cause Analyses, healthcare failure mode and effect analyses, adverse event reporting) for a given organization (U. S. Department of Veterans Affairs National Center for Patient Safety, 2006).

Probabilistic Risk Assessment (PRA): A highly structured process used to identify and weigh the likelihood of undesirable outcomes in order to mitigate the highest-risk failure combinations. PRA takes into account the interrelationship between equipment failures, human errors, at-risk behaviors, and patient factors in complex technical systems (e.g., health care) (Marx, 2005).

Root Cause Analysis (RCA): A structured process for identifying the causal or contributing factors underlying adverse events or other critical incidents (AHRQ Patient Safety Network Glossary, 2006).

Safety Culture: Safety culture (or "culture of safety") refers to a commitment to safety that permeates all levels of an organization, from front-line personnel to executive management. More specifically, "safety culture" calls up a number of features identified in studies of high-reliability organizations, organizations outside of health care with exemplary performance with respect to safety. These features include (1) acknowledgment of the high-risk, error-prone nature of an organization's activities; (2) a blame-free environment where individuals are able to report errors or close calls without fear of reprimand or punishment; (3) an expectation of collaboration across ranks to seek solutions to vulnerabilities; and (4) a willingness on the part of the organization to direct resources for addressing safety concerns (AHRQ Patient Safety Network Glossary, 2006).

Sentinel Event: An unexpected occurrence involving death or serious physical or psychological injury, or the risk thereof. Serious injury specifically includes loss of limb or function. The phrase, "or the risk thereof" includes any process variation for which a recurrence would carry a significant chance of a serious adverse outcome (JCAHO, 2006).

Sharp end: The "sharp end" refers to the personnel or parts of the health care system in direct contact with patients (AHRQ Patient Safety Network Glossary, 2006).

Executive Summary

BACKGROUND

In early 2000, the Institute of Medicine (IOM) published a report entitled *To Err Is Human: Building a Safer Health System*, which highlighted the severity of the *patient safety*[1] problem in the U.S. health care system and mobilized national efforts to improve the safety of the system (IOM, 2000). The IOM called for leadership from the Department of Health and Human Services (DHHS) in reducing *medical errors*, identifying AHRQ as the national focal point for patient safety research and practice improvements. In response to the IOM report, the Quality Interagency Coordination Task Force (QuIC), a collaborative effort among Federal agencies,[2] issued a report in February 2000: *Doing What Counts for Patient Safety: Federal Actions to Reduce Medical Errors and Their Impact* (QuIC, 2000). This report laid out a strategy of more than 100 actions designed to create a national focus on reducing errors, strengthen the patient safety knowledge base, ensure accountability for safe health care delivery, and implement patient safety practices.

Since 2000, the Agency for Healthcare Research and Quality (AHRQ) has had a congressional mandate to take a leadership role in helping health care providers reduce medical errors and improve patient safety. When the U.S. Congress established patient safety as a national priority and gave AHRQ this mandate, it provided AHRQ with funding to support related research and implementation activities. AHRQ has been fulfilling its mandate by developing a comprehensive strategy for supporting expansion of knowledge about the epidemiology of and effective practices for patient safety, and identifying and disseminating the most effective practices for use in the U.S. health care system. The AHRQ patient safety work is one of numerous and important patient safety initiatives being undertaken by a variety of organizations across the country.

The Patient Safety Improvement Corps (PSIC) is a nationwide training program being carried out as part of AHRQ's overall patient safety initiative. The PSIC was designed to improve patient safety in the nation by ultimately providing patient safety training to teams from all U.S. states and the District of Columbia over a three-year period. Operated in partnership by AHRQ and the Department of Veterans Affairs (VA) National Center for Patient Safety (NCPS), the PSIC's primary goal was to improve patient safety by providing the specific knowledge and skills necessary to

- Conduct effective investigations of reports of medical errors (e.g., close calls, errors with and without patient injury) by identifying their root causes with an emphasis on underlying system causes.
- Prepare meaningful reports on the findings.
- Develop and implement sustainable system interventions based on report findings.

---

[1]   Definitions of select patient safety terms that are italicized in this document appear in the Glossary.

[2]   The QuIC is composed of members representing the Departments of Commerce, Defense, Health and Human Services, Labor, State, and Veterans Affairs; Federal Bureau of Prisons; Federal Trade Commission; National Highway Transportation and Safety Administration; Office of Management and Budget; Office of Personnel Management; and the U.S. Coast Guard.

- Measure and evaluate the impact of the safety intervention (i.e., mitigate, reduce, or eliminate the opportunity for error and patient injury).
- Ensure the sustainability of effective interventions by transforming them into standard clinical practice (AHRQ, PSIC Fact Sheet, 2006).

The core content of the annual curriculum was developed by AHRQ based upon the findings of a feasibility study as well as consultation with experts and key stakeholders. AHRQ contracted with the VA NCPS to organize and conduct the training sessions, given the latter organization's experience in implementing patient safety education. Most of the instructors are staff from the NCPS, but the PSIC partners also draw upon outside expertise at AHRQ or in the private sector for some aspects of the program content (e.g., probabilistic risk assessment, just culture, evaluation methods, patient safety indicators, mistake proofing, leading change, patient safety culture, designing for safety).

The annual curriculum was repeated each year, with teams from a portion of the states participating in each training round. When the third training year is completed, AHRQ plans to shift the PSIC to a train-the-trainer model through which it will teach teams how to train others within their state about patient safety skills and tools incorporated in the PSIC program. The goal of the train-the-trainer portion of the PSIC is to broaden the reach of the PSIC to more individuals and organizations throughout the United States.

Each annual training program consists of three one-week sessions in September, January, and May. The training is composed of didactic sessions led by NCPS and other experts, homework and reading assignments to complete between sessions, and a patient safety improvement project that each team conducts in its home organization(s). As required by the interagency agreement (IAA), technical assistance conference calls are offered to the trainees. The VA facilitates these optional, biweekly conference calls, in which trainees may participate if they find them useful. These calls provide a technical assistance support system to PSIC participants and a vehicle for exchange of ideas and experiences among participating teams.

Eligible participants in the PSIC are teams of state staff responsible for patient safety activities and up to two of each state's selected hospital partners (for a total of four participants maximum per state). The original focus of the training was directed towards state staff. Hospital representatives were included in the training at the request of the states participating in the pre-PSIC program conference calls. The PSIC program is tuition-free, and teams selected to participate also are reimbursed for airfare, lodging, per diem, and local travel costs. In addition, each participant receives a library of books and other resource materials.

In the first year of the PSIC (2003–2004), teams representing 15 states completed the program. In the second year (2004–2005), teams representing 21 states completed the program. In some cases, some state-designated Quality Improvement Organizations (QIOs) spearheaded a state team in states where the state departments of health elected not to participate.

Through the training, participants progress from learning basic patient safety principles and concepts in the first session to training in more sophisticated skills, such as statistical techniques for assessing patient risks, in the second session. In the third session, each state team presented its patient safety project and results. All three sessions focus on the practical application of patient safety science, change implementation and management, medical error reporting and analysis, medical/legal issues, and patient safety tools.

EVALUATION APPROACH

The PSIC is an important component of AHRQ's patient safety initiative, which is designed to strengthen the national infrastructure by supporting patient safety improvement activities across the participating states. Therefore, our evaluation focused on this program (1) to provide feedback to AHRQ and the VA on the participants' experience with the program and suggestions for ways to make the program as useful as possible for them, and (2) to assess the extent to which the knowledge and skills gained from the PSIC training have been put to work by the participants in actions for patient safety improvements.

To gather information on these questions, we used a combination of group interviews with participating teams and follow-up interviews with PSIC graduates. (Refer to Appendixes A through C for the interview protocols used.) RAND researchers conducted group interviews with many of the teams during their final training sessions in May of each year (2004 for teams in the first training round and 2005 for teams in the second round). Although we interviewed only a subset of the teams (11 of 15 in 2004, and 12 of 21 in 2005) because of time constraints, those we interviewed had similar perceptions and responses about their experiences with the training. All trainees interviewed in person volunteered to participate; thus the sample is considered a convenience sample.

The individual follow-up telephone interviews were conducted with graduates of the program about 10 months after they completed the PSIC program. In March through May 2005, we conducted these interviews with 38 representatives from the 15 state teams that participated in the first (2003–2004) PSIC training (15 from states and 23 from hospitals). Trainees were not required to participate in the group or individual interviews.

TRAINEE PERCEPTIONS OF THE PSIC TRAINING

In this section, we describe the responses of the PSIC trainees to the training they were provided. We gathered this information from the trainees who participated in the first two PSIC training rounds, in interviews conducted at the final training session in May 2004 and 2005. Therefore, this information represents the trainees' perceptions of the program at the time they were finishing their training. Responses from the trainee teams participating in the first and second PSIC rounds are reported separately, to provide comparisons of the experiences of the two groups. In the discussion, we refer to the two groups as "Year 1" and "Year 2" trainees or participants. We also report separately the perceptions and uses of the program by the staff from state offices and those from hospitals, recognizing their distinct, and often complementary, needs and priorities. As shown in our findings, AHRQ's inclusion of the hospital representatives in the training, as requested by the state participants, has diversified both the scope of knowledge and the practices in the field across both types of organizations.

Team Composition and Formation

As required by AHRQ, the state teams comprised representatives from both the states (e.g., an employee of a state health department) and hospitals. In 2003–2004 (Year 1), participants from the states had a variety of roles (e.g., director of hospital programs, assistant attorney general, epidemiologist), and participants from hospitals tended to be quality improvement and/or risk managers. More so than the Year 1 trainees, the Year 2 trainees from hospitals tended to hold positions with responsibilities directly related to patient safety (e.g., patient safety officer), perhaps reflecting increased national awareness of the importance of patient safety.

Team members from the states tended to be employed by state health departments in a regulatory capacity. A number of team members in Year 2 also were affiliated with QIOs. Based upon the participants we spoke to at the end of their training year, Year 1 team membership remained stable over the course of the year-long training. In Year 2, seven of the 12 teams interviewed reported changes in membership or that some members had to miss some parts of the training. Trainees had learned about the PSIC program in a variety of ways. In Year 1, team formation was typically initiated by one or two individuals who saw an announcement about the program on AHRQ's Web site and approached others about applying; hospitals were more frequently the initiators of the team formation. In Year 2, many individuals had heard about the PSIC and actively tracked the call for applications in the second year. As was required by AHRQ, in both Years 1 and 2, one organization representing the state undertook the actual application process.

Expectations of PSIC Trainees

Year 1 participants entered the program with a cursory-yet-accurate understanding of its purpose and requirements, and a belief that their involvement would be worthwhile. However, they tended to underestimate the amount of reading and homework required, and the magnitude of effort needed to complete the team project.

Expectations of the Year 2 trainees entering the program varied widely: Some knew a great deal about the program; others were not sure of the details. All hoped to learn valuable skills. The majority of second-year participants were aware that the program would be demanding in terms of reading assignments and the team project. They also recognized that as participants in the PSIC, they were expected to share what they learned with colleagues at home.

Prior Knowledge and Experience of Trainees

The patient safety knowledge and experience level of Year 1 participants varied widely. Some had used or taught about patient safety tools, designed interventions for improvement, and evaluated such interventions; others were being exposed to these concepts for the first time. In Year 2, most trainees had a general understanding of patient safety issues (91 percent) but were not as familiar with tools and interventions (57 and 68 percent, respectively).

Content of the PSIC Training

Both groups of trainees interviewed felt that the content of the training was targeted at the appropriate level. Of the skills and tools taught during the course, the ones used most often by the trainees were Root Cause Analysis (RCA) and Healthcare Failure Mode and Effects Analysis (HFMEA); this was especially true in Year 1, reflecting the initial emphasis for teams to focus on these two methods in their projects, the topics of which were selected by the participants. (In Year 2, trainees were encouraged to tackle any patient safety project topic of their choice with the expectation that one of the tools or methods provided in their training would be used to complete the projects.) The networking aspects of the course were also valued highly. The majority of trainees took the responsibility of sharing information with colleagues at home very seriously, and trainees were already taking steps on this front during the training year.

As summarized in Table S.1, most of the Year 2 participants we interviewed reported having a high skill level in major patient safety areas by the end of the Year 2 PSIC training session. On a scale of 1 to 5 (with 5 being the highest skill level), all but a small percentage of Year 2 trainees rated themselves at skill level 4 or 5. These participants felt that their team had been successful in conducting their PSIC project despite implementation challenges.

(Comparable data were not collected for Year 1 trainees. Given that the evaluation goals of the first year were exploratory, we tracked only the initial experiences and dynamics of the PSIC program. In subsequent years, we increasingly tracked results and outcomes in a more quantifiable manner.)

Table S.1
Skill Levels Reported by Year 2 Trainees at the End of the Year 2 PSIC Training

Skill Area	Percentage Reporting Skill Level (N=45)				
	1 (None)	2	3	4	5 (Very skilled)
Select the appropriate tool(s) to investigate an error or near miss.	0%	0%	9%	56%	36%
Conduct an investigation of a medical error or near miss and prepare reports based on your findings.	0	0	11	56	33
Develop an intervention based on the findings from your investigation.	0	0	16	62	22
Measure and evaluate the impact of the safety intervention you developed.	2	0	16	58	24
Translate patient safety interventions into standard clinical practice.	0	2	22	60	16

NOTE: Percentages within a category may not sum to 100 percent due to rounding error. Comparable data were not collected for Year 1 trainees. Given that the evaluation goals of the first year were exploratory, we tracked only the initial experiences and dynamics of the PSIC program. In subsequent years, we increasingly tracked results and outcomes in a more quantifiable manner.

Although the team projects were diverse in both years, the nature of the projects differed between the two years: At the encouragement of the AHRQ/VA partnership, Year 1 topics included methods presented in the previous training (especially RCA and HFMEA) to solve patient safety challenges and to reinforce the use of and familiarity with the concepts and tools included in the PSIC. Year 2 topics were approached with less emphasis on using RCA and HFMEA, and teams were encouraged to use any of the skills/tools to tackle their real-world problems, such as assessing the patient safety culture. Teams in both years identified many challenges in reaching their project goals. Challenges reported by the Year 1 trainees included initial distrust between hospitals and state regulators. The AHRQ/VA partnership anticipated this issue and hoped it would be overcome with a training program that included teams composed of both state and hospital staff, and focused on preventing harm to patients—a common goal across all trainees. Other challenges reported by Year 1 trainees were lack of patient safety culture in trainees' home organizations, lack of home organization resources, geographic distance between PSIC team members, and lack of full support for the project from the state or the corporate executive officer (CEO), despite the PSIC requirement of official affirmation of CEO support. (CEO involvement was required as part of the application process in the form of a signed commitment letter as well as participation in a telephone call to learn about their employees' participation in the PSIC and its impact on the organization.) The Year 2 trainees reported challenges of balancing PSIC project work with other job commitments and of determining the topic and scope of the team project, lack of accountability at home institution(s) for engagement in the PSIC project, and of organizing a team that was newly formed and represented multiple home organizations with no formal incentives to complete a project.

When asked how to improve the program content, the Year 1 trainees suggested more hands-on exercises, more direction about practical interventions, and more time for discussion among themselves to get to know each other and share experiences. The Year 2 trainees suggested the addition of more information on reporting systems, patient safety leadership, patient safety in long-term care and nursing home facilities, the business case for patient safety, and positive corrective actions, among others. Trainees from both years also suggested that the VA and AHRQ actively recruit more sharp-end clinicians (e.g., MDs, RNs) to participate in the training. In addition, they felt that attendance at the PSIC training by representatives from the Centers for Medicaid and Medicare Services (CMS) and the Joint Commission on Accreditation of Healthcare Organizations (JCAHO) would be useful to increase their awareness of the importance of a "just culture" rather than a "blame" environment, and also to gain additional perspective on how their policies affect providers' ability to pursue patient safety improvements.

Although the Year 2 trainee group was larger than the Year 1 group, the training ran smoothly and with no apparent effects of having a larger number of participants. In fact, the larger group appeared to provide more networking opportunities and more exposure to diverse projects and experiences.

Use of the PSIC Training

In Year 1 of the program, trainees used the skills and tools taught through the PSIC— especially RCAs, HFMEAs, and reporting systems—in real time as the training progressed and shared them with others throughout the course of the program. In Year 2, RCA and HFMEA remained important, but the survey on patient safety culture and the materials on a just culture replaced reporting systems in use by participants—likely due to a more widespread focus on using any tool presented up to that point, rather than an emphasis on RCA and HFMEA as was posed in Year 1. Trainees from both years also reported that they had implemented initiatives as a result of the PSIC. Key barriers to using the PSIC skills and tools on a regular basis at their home organizations as reported by trainees included lack of time, too few staff, and inadequate funding in their home organizations

Participants in the Year 1 PSIC training expressed increased confidence and a more in-depth appreciation of the complexities of patient safety coming out of the program, but they underscored a need for continued training beyond the end of the third week of training. The Year 2 trainees had similar comments, but typically those in clinical settings with more opportunities to practice PSIC-learned methods felt more confident than others.

FEEDBACK ON THE PSIC EXPERIENCE ONE YEAR LATER

In this section, we summarize the findings of the individual interviews conducted with the Year 1 PSIC trainees one year after they completed their training. We asked them to consider in hindsight the value of their experience and to identify how they had put their training to work during the past year. For many of the topics, we report separately the feedback by the state and hospital participants, recognizing their distinct, and often complementary, needs and priorities. As shown in our findings, the inclusion of the hospital representatives in the training, which was requested by states as part of the pre-PSIC program formulation, expanded both the scope of knowledge and the practices in the field across both types of organizations.

Attendance and Support Needed to Attend PSIC Training

Attendance across all three training weeks was strong, and the continuity of team membership during the training year was reasonably steady. The majority of participants (89 percent) felt that they received adequate support from their home institutions to attend the sessions and carry out the team project. However, they also mentioned that the time to do reading assignments and team project work was often an "add-on" to their normal workloads. Trainees encouraged any organization contemplating participation in the PSIC to be receptive to the knowledge that participants bring from the course and to realize the intensity of the commitment of staff time when signing up for the PSIC. We note that this organizational support differs from the issue reported previously regarding inadequate CEO support for the teams conducting their PSIC project within their organizations, which involves a higher level of commitment than sending them for training.

Usefulness of the PSIC Tools One Year Later

One year after their PSIC training ended, Year 1 participants reported that the training had been most useful to them for learning about RCA (95 percent), HFMEA (95 percent), human factors engineering (92 percent), and the reporting of adverse events and near misses (92 percent). Other tools they found fairly useful were the VA's Safety Assessment Code (SAC) (84 percent) and identifying high-alert medications (71 percent). Hospital representatives most often reported using in daily practice the tools and skills related to RCA (87 percent), human factors engineering (83 percent), and reporting of adverse events and near misses (78 percent). Similarly, state representatives said they tended to actually use in daily practice the reporting of adverse event tools and skills (80 percent); they also frequently use the tools to identify high-alert medications (60 percent) and to analyze patient safety data (60 percent). Additionally, participants viewed the networking opportunities and first-hand experience of hospitals and states working collaboratively on patient safety issues as equally important PSIC tools and skills. To help them increase their use of the tools more generally, trainees said additional training and hands-on exercises after the end of the PSIC program would be beneficial, as would periodic refresher courses and literature updates. Across the board, trainees valued the consultative services of the VA and AHRQ, as well as the extensive library provided to each PSIC participant.

Impact of the PSIC on Patient Safety Actions in the First Year Following Training According to Year 1 Trainees

One year later, the PSIC training was reported to have had a substantial impact on patient safety actions taken by states and hospitals participating in the Year 1 training. As shown in the interview responses summarized in Tables S.2 for states and S.3 for hospitals, a variety of specific patient safety actions had been taken by states and hospitals within the first year following their training.

Table S.2
Influence of PSIC Training on Patient Safety Actions by States,
Reported by Year 1 PSIC Trainees One Year Following the Training

Patient Safety Action	Percentage Responding "yes" ($N = 15$)
Initiation of or influence on regulation(s) or legislation	47%
Modification of hospital oversight procedures when an adverse event occurs (e.g., change content of Root Cause Analysis)	47 *
Modification of an existing state reporting system to improve how it captures patient safety issues or how information is reported to others	33
Creation of a statewide reporting system	20
New membership in or formation of a patient safety coalition of stakeholders	20

* For 7 percent of the respondents, this question was not applicable, not relevant to the respondent's type of organization or role within that organization, or the respondent could not answer the question.

Almost half of the 15 states (47 percent) reported they have used information gained through the PSIC training to initiate or influence legislation, or to modify adverse event oversight procedures. They also have used it in their work to improve existing state reporting systems (33 percent) or create new reporting systems (20 percent). The training also has contributed to efforts by 20 percent of the states to join or form patient safety coalitions.

The hospital representatives also said that the PSIC training was an important factor in modifications they have made to adverse event oversight procedures (83 percent), to promote patient safety culture (78 percent), and to share data across organizations in an effort to better understand causes of error (52 percent). The training also contributed to changes made by hospitals in review of adverse events (48 percent) and creation of institutional adverse event reporting systems (30 percent).

Table S.3
Influence of PSIC Training on Patient Safety Actions by Hospitals,
Reported by First Year 2003–2004 Trainees One Year Following PSIC Training

Patient Safety Action	Percentage Responding "yes" (N = 23)
Modification of processes to review/analyze adverse events or errors	83% *
Promotion of patient safety culture	78 *
Sharing data across organizations to better understand causes of error	52
Other changes in review of adverse events	48
Other state- or organization-wide initiatives	48 *
New membership in or formation of a patient safety group of stakeholders	35
Creation of institutional adverse event reporting system	30

* For 4 percent of the respondents, this question was not applicable, not relevant to the respondent's type of organization or role within that organization, or the respondent could not answer the question.

Contact with PSIC Colleagues, AHRQ, and VA After Year 1 Training's End

About three-quarters of the Year 1 PSIC trainees interviewed had communicated with their own PSIC team members during the year following the PSIC training, and nearly two-thirds had contacted the VA during this same period. To a lesser degree, they also remained in contact with other PSIC teams (39 percent). Contact with AHRQ was the least frequent, with approximately one-third of the trainees interviewed having contacted AHRQ since the end of training. Proportionately more hospital than state representatives tended to initiate contact with others after the end of the training. Both hospital and state representatives noted the value of having peers to consult with, and they underscored their appreciation for the assistance of the VA and AHRQ staff.

Helpfulness of PSIC Training and Advice to Others

Overall, 92 percent of the Year 1 participants praised the PSIC training one year after it ended, giving it ratings of 7 points or higher on a 10-point scale. More specifically, as shown in Figure S.1, all but a small percentage of the trainees rated highly the helpfulness of the training in improving processes to monitor and improve patient safety, although the state representatives rated its helpfulness somewhat higher than did the hospital representatives. An estimated 60 percent of the state representatives rated the program at 9 to 10 on a 10-point scale, whereas approximately half of the hospital representatives gave it that rating.

The majority of the Year 1 trainees also said that they would recommend enthusiastically the PSIC training to other states (89 percent) and hospitals (92 percent). Participants advised those contemplating participation to assemble a diverse team of senior management, front-line clinical staff (i.e., those providing direct patient care), and those involved directly in patient safety efforts from both hospitals and states (e.g., patient safety officers, risk managers).

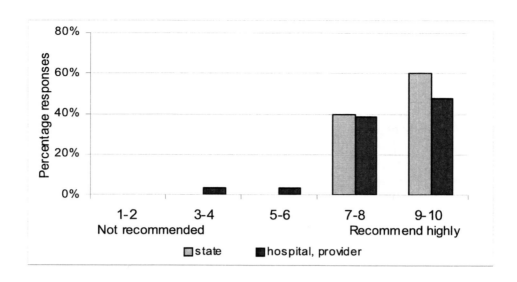

Figure S.1 Assessment by First-Year Trainees of the Helpfulness of PSIC Training in Improving Processes to Monitor and Improve Patient Safety

Past Experience and Interest in Training Others

In the year since the training's end, 87 percent of the Year 1 PSIC graduates said that they had trained others in the use of patient safety skills and tools. A slightly larger portion of hospital representatives (91 percent) had trained others than had state representatives (80 percent). A significant majority also said that they were willing to serve as trainers to others in their state in the future (82 percent). To do such training in a more formal capacity, trainees noted that they would need assistance from AHRQ and the VA for financing, course content, and logistics. The AHRQ/VA partnership anticipated some of these needs and plans to address them through its train-the-trainer course to be held after the completion of the Year 3 PSIC training. The interest expressed by these PSIC graduates in training others suggests that there is some demand for this course. Those who had not trained any staff, or who were not interested in doing so in the future, typically did not feel competent to do so or felt such training was not relevant to their current positions.

Need for Further Training/Refresher Course

One year after finishing PSIC training, 92 percent of the Year 1 participants were interested in additional patient safety training or some sort of refresher course. Suggestions for content ranged from consultation on individual projects to "big-picture" updates on new patient safety literature and tools. A preference was expressed for interactive sessions and a program length of one or two days.

DISCUSSION OF FINDINGS

Overall, the short- and longer-term experiences reported in the interviews by the first two groups of PSIC trainees were very positive. Participants said that they valued the broad perspective they gained about patient safety and the tools and skills they learned and were continuing to use. They appreciated and continued to draw upon the technical aspects of the training, the hands-on exercises, the knowledge gained through their own and other teams' projects, and the extensive reference materials and library provided as part of the program. Additionally, they continue to view the networking opportunities created by the PSIC training as a significant resource.

Significantly, according to participant responses, there are strong indications that the PSIC program in both years has contributed to actions in the field to improve patient safety. These findings suggest that the PSIC is making important contributions toward building a national infrastructure to support implementation of effective patient safety practices.

During the Year 1 training, many state and hospital representatives shared information and materials with colleagues back home, and they were pushing to implement patient safety initiatives in a variety of areas, many directly related to their PSIC team project. One year later, these PSIC graduates reported that they had used many of the PSIC skills and tools to make meaningful changes on a variety of patient safety fronts. Their newly gained knowledge and enthusiasm, coupled with the general climate of increased attention on patient safety issues across the nation in the year after their training, has created a fertile ground for change and improvement.

Similarly, the Year 2 PSIC graduates have mastered a set of skills, and have been sharing the skills and tools learned in the training with others in their immediate organizations, as well as more broadly in their local communities and across their states. They have drawn upon these resources to launch new patient safety initiatives and to improve existing ones.

Notably, there was an early awareness among the Year 2 trainees of the necessity for somewhat adversarial parties to collaborate (e.g., hospital staff versus state regulators). Part of this change from the previous year probably is attributable to the increased interest in and awareness of patient safety issues nationally, and the ensuing realization by these parties of the benefits of collaboration. According to the attendees, the PSIC has played an instrumental role in changing attitudes. The experiences of the Year 1 group, coupled with the national trend of increasing awareness of patient safety issues, seems to have paved the way for easier interactions in the Year 2 group.

Trainees noted some barriers that created challenges for their ability to make changes at home. Such barriers ranged from lack of resources (e.g., time, funds) to lack of a patient safety culture at their home institutions. They also underscored a need for continued training beyond the end of the third week of the PSIC course, and they voiced the need to train larger, more-diverse teams that include sharp-end clinicians, high-level decisionmakers (e.g., CEOs), and senior staff from both hospitals and states. We note that AHRQ specifically did not target the CEOs for training because many patient safety training options already existed for them through other programs geared to health care executives.

In view of our assessment of the PSIC at this time, we offer the following suggestions for AHRQ action in crafting any future PSIC activities:

- Building upon the successful PSIC training that has reached the important audience of front-line hospital and state-level staff, AHRQ should consider alternative education models to engage key decisionmakers who make patient safety improvements happen, for whom other training programs do not already exist (e.g., state legislators).

- AHRQ should provide continued limited support to the PSIC graduates to help them remain engaged in patient safety issues, keep their skills and knowledge current, and encourage cross-fertilization among the PSIC graduates, as well as between graduates and others in the field, such as content experts and front-line clinical people with experience in implementing patient safety improvements.

Acknowledgments

We gratefully acknowledge the participation of numerous people in the evaluation of the Patient Safety Improvement Corps. The individuals who were PSIC trainees willingly have provided their time to participate in individual interviews and focus groups, providing valuable information and insights about the PSIC and their use of the training they received.

Representatives from AHRQ and the VA also contributed, through their careful review of interview protocols to help ensure that the evaluation addressed pertinent topics and issues. In particular, we thank Marge Keyes, the AHRQ project officer for the PSIC, and Caryl Lee, the VA lead for the conduct of PSIC training, for their commitment to the project and to the evaluation process. In addition, James Battles, the AHRQ project officer for the overall patient safety evaluation, has been instrumental in guiding the formation and execution of the evaluation. We also thank our RAND colleagues Rebecca Shaw, Chau Pham, Stephanie Taylor, and Stacy Fitzsimmons for their indispensable contributions to our data-collection and data-analysis processes.

Chapter 1
Introduction

BACKGROUND

In early 2000, the Institute of Medicine (IOM) published a report entitled *To Err Is Human: Building a Safer Health System*, which mobilized national efforts to improve the safety of the U.S. health care system (IOM, 2000). The IOM called for leadership from the Department of Health and Human Services (DHHS) in reducing medical errors, identifying AHRQ as the national focal point for *patient safety* research and practice improvements. In response to the IOM report, the Quality Interagency Coordination Task Force (QuIC), a collaborative effort among federal agencies,[1] issued a report in February 2000: *Doing What Counts for Patient Safety: Federal Actions to Reduce Medical Errors and Their Impact* (QuIC, 2000). This report laid out a strategy of more than 100 actions designed to create a national focus on reducing errors, strengthen the patient safety knowledge base, ensure accountability for safe health care delivery, and implement patient safety practices.

Since 2000, the Agency for Healthcare Research and Quality (AHRQ) has had a congressional mandate to take a leadership role in helping health care providers reduce medical errors and improve patient safety. When the U.S. Congress established patient safety as a national priority and gave AHRQ this mandate, it provided AHRQ with funding to support related research and implementation activities. AHRQ has been fulfilling its mandate by developing a comprehensive strategy for supporting expansion of knowledge about the epidemiology of and effective practices for patient safety, and identifying and disseminating the most effective practices for use in the U.S. health care system. The AHRQ patient safety work is one of numerous and important patient safety initiatives being undertaken by a variety of organizations across the country. The Patient Safety Improvement Corps (PSIC) is a nationwide training program being carried out as part of AHRQ's overall patient safety initiative. It is funded by AHRQ with $7 million over four years, and is operated collaboratively by AHRQ and the VA National Center for Patient Safety (NCPS) (which is headquartered in Ann Arbor, Michigan).

THE TRAINING PROGRAM DESIGN

The PSIC has as its purpose to improve patient safety in the nation by increasing the number and capacity of health care professionals with core patient safety knowledge and skills to

- Conduct effective investigations of reports of medical errors (e.g., close calls, errors with and without patient injury) by identifying their root causes with an emphasis on underlying system causes.
- Prepare meaningful reports on the findings.
- Develop and implement sustainable system interventions based on report findings.

---

[1] The QuIC is composed of members representing the Departments of Commerce, Defense, Health and Human Services, Labor, State, and Veterans Affairs; Federal Bureau of Prisons; Federal Trade Commission; National Highway Transportation and Safety Administration; Office of Management and Budget; Office of Personnel Management; and the U.S. Coast Guard.

- Measure and evaluate the impact of the safety intervention (i.e., mitigate, reduce, or eliminate the opportunity for error and patient injury).
- Ensure the sustainability of effective interventions by transforming them into standard clinical practice (AHRQ, PSIC Fact Sheet, 2006).

The PSIC was designed to ultimately provide patient safety training to teams from all U.S. states and the District of Columbia over a three-year period. The year-long program consists of three one-week sessions in September, January, and May and is repeated each year with teams from a portion of the states participating in each training round. The core content of the annual training curriculum was developed by AHRQ based upon the findings of a feasibility study as well as consultation with experts and key stakeholders (e.g., representatives from states and hospitals). Through an interagency agreement, AHRQ contracted with the VA NCPS to implement the training, given the latter organization's experience in implementing patient safety education. The interagency agreement (IAA) included specific requirements pertaining to the course content, selection of instructors, provision of technical assistance and a library of materials for the trainees, identification of the target audience, and evaluation of the program by participants and their employers. Most of the instructors are staff from the NCPS, but the PSIC partners also draw upon outside expertise at AHRQ or in the private sector for some aspects of the program content (e.g., probabilistic risk assessment, just culture, evaluation methods, patient safety indicators, mistake proofing, leading change, patient safety culture, designing for safety).

The VA conducts the training, which is composed of didactic sessions, homework and reading assignments to complete between sessions, and team patient safety projects. The teams are to identify their projects by the first (September) training session, and complete their project plan by the second (December) session. They work on the project at home for the remainder of the training year, and the third (May) session is dedicated to reports on the project results in addition to training on various new patient safety topics. Between training sessions, the VA NCPS also facilitates biweekly, optional conference calls to provide technical assistance as needed.

Participants eligible for this program are teams of state staff in the field (e.g., patient safety officers or those responsible for patient safety reporting and analysis as well as for intervention initiatives) and the state's selected hospital partners. The original focus of the training was on state staff, to help them develop patient safety knowledge and skills. Hospital representatives were included in the training at the request of the state participants as expressed in their pre-PSIC conference calls with AHRQ.

The PSIC program is tuition-free (i.e., teams selected to participate are reimbursed for airfare, lodging, per diem, and local travel costs). Each participant also is given a large set of books and resources, including a notebook containing all of the slides and handouts for each session, flip books on Root Cause Analysis (RCA) and Healthcare Failure Mode and Effects Analysis (HFMEA), and support materials for other specific tools. In terms of the application process, only states (i.e., individuals representing state-level organizations such as state health departments) may submit applications, but the state applications may include up to two hospital partners as selected by the state (for a maximum of four participants per state).

In 2003–2004—Year 1 of the PSIC—15 state teams completed the program; another 21 state teams completed the program in 2004–2005 (Year 2). Table 1.1 identifies the states participating in the first two years of the program.

Table 1.1
Summary of Year 1 and Year 2 PSIC Trainees

PSIC Training Year	Number of Participating States	List of Participating States
2003–2004 (Year 1)	15	Alaska, Connecticut, Maryland, Massachusetts, Minnesota, Missouri, New York, North Carolina, Oregon, Pennsylvania, Rhode Island, Texas, Utah, Virginia, Wisconsin
2004–2005 (Year 2)	21	California, District of Columbia, Florida, Georgia, Hawaii, Idaho, Indiana, Kentucky, Maryland, Massachusetts, Michigan, Mississippi, Nebraska, New Jersey, North Dakota, Ohio, South Dakota, Tennessee, Vermont, Washington, West Virginia

NOTE: Two states, Maryland and Massachusetts, sent teams in both 2003–2004 and 2004-2005.

The PSIC training focuses on the practical application of patient safety science and techniques. Each session builds on what was taught during the previous one. In addition, each state team carries out a patient safety project, the results of which are presented at the third training session in May. The following are examples of topics covered during the course of the one-year training:

- overview of patient safety
- state medical legal issues
- state confidentiality issues
- patient safety and human factors engineering
- leadership strategies used by high-reliability organizations
- simulations for training
- Root Cause Analysis
- prioritizing adverse events and close calls
- risk assessment tools and methods
- actions and outcome measures
- cause and effect diagramming
- Healthcare Failure Mode and Effects Analysis process.

Between the second and third weeks of each annual program, the VA NCPS facilitates biweekly, optional conference calls in which participants may participate if they find them useful. These calls provide a technical assistance support system to PSIC participants and a vehicle for exchange of ideas and experiences among participating teams. Updated information regarding upcoming patient safety conferences is also disseminated via the conference calls.

When the third training year is completed and teams from all U.S. states and the District of Columbia have been trained, AHRQ plans to shift the PSIC to a train-the-trainer model through which it will teach teams how to train others within their state about patient safety skills and tools. The goal of the train-the-trainer portion of the PSIC is to broaden the reach of the PSIC to more individuals and organizations.

EVALUATING THE PSIC ROLE IN THE AHRQ PATIENT SAFETY INITIATIVE

AHRQ contracted with RAND in September 2002 to serve as the evaluation center for its national patient safety initiative. The evaluation center is responsible for performing a longitudinal evaluation of the full scope of AHRQ's patient safety activities and for providing regular feedback to support the continuing improvement of this initiative over the four-year project period.

The PSIC is an important component of AHRQ's patient safety initiative, which is designed to strengthen the national infrastructure by supporting patient safety improvement activities across the participating states. Therefore, RAND's evaluation focused on this program for two reasons: (1) to provide feedback to AHRQ and the VA on the participants' experience with the program and suggestions for ways to make the program as useful as possible for them and (2) to assess the extent to which the knowledge and skills gained from the PSIC training have been put to work by the participants in actions for patient safety improvements.

This evaluation is designed as a formative program evaluation: It tracks a program during its operation to learn from its experiences and improve future program activities. In particular, it is important for this type of evaluation to document the experiences and perceptions of the key stakeholders involved in the program. Information on the evaluation questions was gathered using a combination of group interviews with the teams and follow-up interviews with individual participants after they had completed the PSIC training. This process allowed us to gather longitudinal data on the experiences of the Year 1 trainees, during and after their training. (Refer to Appendixes A through C for the interview protocols used in these two types of interviews.)

The group interviews were conducted during the third and final week of training in May of each year (2004 and 2005). In May 2004, we conducted team interviews with 11 of the 15 states participating in the first PSIC round at their final training session. Similarly, in May 2005, we conducted team interviews with 12 of the 21 states participating in the second PSIC round. A RAND researcher led the discussion with members of each state team, using a structured interview protocol. A similar interview protocol was used each year. However, comparable data were not collected for Year 1 trainees. Given that the evaluation goals of the first year were exploratory, we tracked only the initial experiences and dynamics of the PSIC program. In subsequent years, we increasingly tracked results and outcomes in a more quantifiable manner.

All trainees interviewed in person volunteered to participate; thus the sample is considered a convenience sample. We did not interview all of the teams because of time constraints during the session, and some teams did not want to participate. The teams we interviewed had similar perceptions and feedback about their experiences with the training, giving us confidence in the validity of the information obtained from the interviews.

The individual follow-up telephone interviews with graduates of Year 1 of the program were conducted about 10 months after they completed the PSIC program. In March through May 2005, we conducted these interviews with 38 representatives from the 15 state teams that participated in the 2003–2004 PSIC (i.e., Year 1) training (15 from states and 23 from hospitals). Interviews also were conducted with the Year 2 group in spring 2006.

The use of group and individual interviews is the strongest method to achieve the information goals of the evaluation. However, interview data have the limitation of being self-reported information, which unavoidably reflects the biases of the stakeholders being interviewed. Additionally, trainees were not required to participate in the group or individual interviews. We attempted to minimize sampling bias by interviewing as many of the teams and individual participants as possible. However, we were not able to address bias embedded in self-reported data, which could be done only by using observational techniques or through review of pertinent materials that document the actions being reported. It is for this reason that we present and interpret the evaluation information as representing the viewpoints of the PSIC trainees, rather than as objectively observed facts.

CONTENTS OF THIS REPORT

This report presents the findings of RAND's evaluation of the PSIC as of September 2005. In this Chapter, an overview is provided of the PSIC training program design and participants, as well as our evaluation approach and methods. Chapter 2 presents the evaluation results regarding the experiences and perceptions of the first group of PSIC trainees, and Chapter 3 presents those results for the second trainee group. In Chapter 3, we also discuss similarities and differences between the Year 1 and Year 2 trainee groups in their training experiences and use of what they have learned. Chapter 4 presents our conclusions regarding the PSIC and its contribution to the overall AHRQ patient safety initiative, along with suggestions to AHRQ for actions to further strengthen the training and for future program design and activities.

Chapter 2
Lessons from the First-Year PSIC Trainees

OVERVIEW OF FINDINGS

Overall, the Year 1 PSIC trainees (2003–2004) positively evaluated their PSIC experience—an assessment provided in the interviews conducted during the third and final training session for this group and reinforced one year later in the telephone interviews. Both at the time of the training and one year later, Year 1 PSIC participants valued the tools and skills they learned and were continuing to use, many as a day-to-day part of their positions. They appreciated and continued to draw upon the technical aspects of the training, the hands-on exercises—especially the knowledge gained through their own and other teams' projects, and the extensive reference materials and library provided as part of the program. In particular, participants valued the instruction on RCA, HFMEA, human factors engineering, and the reporting of adverse events and/or near misses. Additionally, they continued to view the course's networking opportunities and the broader perspective they gained about patient safety as useful resources.

The trainee reports offer some evidence that the PSIC program has facilitated changes to improve patient safety within the organizations of the PSIC participants. As this program completes training for teams across all U.S. states and the District of Columbia, it is contributing to a national infrastructure of personnel trained in patient safety, to help support effective patient safety practices. During the training year, many state and hospital representatives shared information and materials with colleagues at their home institutions, and they were pushing to implement patient safety initiatives in a variety of areas, many directly related to their PSIC team project. One year later, the Year 1 PSIC graduates had used many of the PSIC skills and tools to make meaningful changes on a variety of patient safety fronts, including but not limited to state regulations or legislation, analysis and reporting of adverse events, existing reporting system, composition of stakeholder coalitions, and patient safety culture. There was a clear conviction among many PSIC trainees that the PSIC had "helped them get the ball rolling." Their newly gained knowledge and enthusiasm, coupled with the general climate of increased attention on patient safety issues across the nation in the year after their training, have created a fertile ground for change and improvement.

Trainees noted some barriers to their ability to make changes after the program's end. Such barriers ranged from lack of resources (e.g., time, funds) to lack of a patient safety culture at their home institutions. PSIC participants also underscored a need for continued training beyond the end of the third PSIC session—both for themselves and for colleagues at home—in the form of refresher courses with hands-on exercises, as well as updates about new literature and effective interventions. Participants also voiced the need to have larger, more diverse teams that include sharp-end clinicians, senior staff from hospitals and from states, and representatives from both the Centers for Medicare & Medicaid Services (CMS) and the Joint Commission on Accreditation of Healthcare Organizations (JCAHO) to bring about change more rapidly. However, despite such shortcomings, the overwhelming majority of the Year 1 participants—both at the time of the training and with one year of hindsight—said that they would recommend the course to others.

In the remainder of this chapter, we present the detailed findings that contribute to these summary assessments by the Year 1 PSIC trainees.

FINDINGS FROM THE MAY 2004 TEAM INTERVIEWS

In May 2004, during the final week of Year 1 of the PSIC training program, RAND researchers interviewed 11 of the 15 participating state teams to

- assess their experiences with the training
- evaluate how they were applying to their day-to-day work what they had learned through the PSIC training
- solicit their thoughts for improving the program.

The teams that were interviewed volunteered to be interviewed by signing up at the beginning of the third PSIC training week. We did not interview all of the teams because of time constraints during the session, and some teams did not want to participate. The teams we interviewed had similar perceptions of and feedback about their experiences with the training, giving us confidence in the validity of the information obtained from the interviews. However, some opinions held by the teams not interviewed may not have been captured. Three RAND researchers interviewed one or more teams at the end of each of the three full days of training using a structured protocol containing primarily open-ended questions (see Appendix A for the interview protocol). The findings from these team interviews are presented below.

Because these were group interviews, with open-ended questions, the synthesis of the interview results is, of necessity, qualitative in nature. By contrast, for the one-year follow-up interviews with individual participants, we were able to obtain more-structured information that could be tabulated and presented in tables. (See Appendix B for the interview protocol.) These follow-up results are presented in the next main section of this chapter ("Feedback on the PSIC Experience One Year Later"). In the following subsections, we summarize feedback on team composition and formation; expectations of and satisfaction with the PSIC training; prior knowledge and experience of participants; content of the training; and the short-term impact of the training.

Team Composition and Formation

- *Key points*: The majority of teams report that they functioned well together and their composition did not change over the course of the training year.

As required by AHRQ, the state teams comprised representatives from both the state and hospitals. Participants from the state had a variety of roles, including managing state licensing programs, training hospital surveyors and educators, reviewing state patient safety programs, ensuring compliance with patient safety regulations and reporting requirements, conducting RCAs of reported adverse events, investigating complaints, and writing rules for state patient safety legislation. Participants from hospitals tended to be the patient safety officer (or similarly titled individual responsible for patient safety-related quality improvement); they ranged from front-line, practicing clinicians to administrators. Many of these hospital-affiliated individuals were responsible for training and education, and many served on one or more patient safety-related committees or boards within their institution and broader community.

The 11 teams interviewed varied in their cohesiveness, according to the teams' self-assessments of how well they worked together. The majority seemed to get along well and function as a team. However, because, historically, hospitals did not talk openly with regulators, a few teams suffered initially from distrust among the partners (e.g., hospitals and regulators viewing each other as "the adversary"). Some teams also suffered from the "free rider problem" (e.g., one or two team members feeling as though they were doing all the work on the team project). In Year 1, team formation was typically initiated by one or two individuals who saw an announcement about the program on AHRQ's Web site and approached others about applying. Across the 11 teams interviewed, hospitals were more frequently the initiators of the team formation. However, as was required by AHRQ, state representatives spearheaded the actual application process.

For the most part, the configuration of the teams interviewed did not change over the course of the year-long training. Occasionally, one team member had to miss a session (due to family matters, primarily), and in a few instances there was staff turnover, but these cases were rare. When they did occur, a temporary or replacement filled in for the missing team member.

Expectations of and Satisfaction with the PSIC Training

- *Key points*: Most participants entered the program with a cursory-yet-accurate understanding of the program's purpose and requirements, and a belief that their involvement would be worthwhile. The main area of misunderstanding was in the amount of reading and homework required, and the magnitude of effort needed to complete the team project. Despite this misunderstanding, trainees were enthusiastic about the program.

The initial trainee expectations for the program were mixed. Before the PSIC training, many participants were not sure what to expect but believed the sessions would be an important learning opportunity. The majority of participants were aware that they were required to work on a team project, but they were not sure of specifics. Most knew that fostering a partnership between the states and hospitals was an important goal. A few participants had very specific expectations about the skills they wanted to walk away with (e.g., confidence about doing an RCA or HFMEA, knowledge about implementing an adverse event reporting system).

On the whole, participants felt that their expectations were met and often exceeded, and many were enthusiastic about the PSIC training. They specifically appreciated the following:

- networking opportunities
- library of patient safety resources
- access to experts in the field; increased ability to teach best practices
- enhanced understanding of and relationships between states and hospitals.

However, many participants did not realize the amount of reading and homework required, and they found it challenging to complete assignments in addition to their normal work responsibilities. Some also did not fully anticipate the time required to carry out the team project.

On some teams, the state members were unsure how they fit into the team or could incorporate the skills and tools into their daily work, despite their having the lead in inviting the hospital representatives to participate. Some state members reported that much of the course is geared to people on the front lines who would be using the tools (e.g., RCAs, HFMEAs), but they would not be using them on a regular basis. Although they said they valued the exposure to these tools, they felt a bit removed from the exercises using the tools because they do not see themselves ever using them. In addition, teams that were formed at the encouragement of hospitals often were comprised of state representatives who were unfamiliar with patient safety issues at the outset of the PSIC program, meaning they had more "catching up" to do in terms of developing a background in patient safety.

Despite these issues, many teams noted in the interviews that the state's involvement led to enhanced relationships and awareness that "the state is not the enemy." Such enhanced relationships were an explicit goal of AHRQ, which designed the PSIC program to include individuals functioning in a wide variety of roles related to patient safety. In particular and at the request of states, AHRQ included a requirement for hospital participation on each state team with the aim of fostering relationships between state regulators and hospitals for the purpose of improving patient safety. Finally, participants noted that it was important to have some basic knowledge of patient safety issues before starting the training—knowledge that varied across participants. Those who did not have much depth of knowledge said the early part of the training was difficult for them.

Prior Knowledge and Experience of Participants

- *Key points*: Both knowledge of patient safety and the experience level of individuals coming into the program varied widely. Regardless of their level, trainees appreciated the PSIC instruction and the opportunity to immediately practice what they learned through hands-on exercises. More-sophisticated participants valued fine-tuning their skills and knowledge of tools.

In terms of general knowledge of medical error, patient safety, and the risks and hazards in the system leading to patient injury, the experience of individual team members prior to participation in the PSIC varied. Many were familiar with basic patient safety issues; quite a few were at least familiar with or had read the Institute of Medicine's (IOM's) report *To Err Is Human* (IOM, 2000); some had extensive, direct experience because of their professional roles within their organizations.

Prior to participation in the PSIC, trainees' experience with tools used to investigate near misses, medical errors, and patient injury also varied widely. Some participants had minimal knowledge of the tools, whereas others had been using such tools as RCA and HFMEA for years and had even taught others how to use them. In most cases, even if an individual knew a significant amount about a given tool, he/she said it was useful to hear about it again from a new instructor and, especially, to be exposed to the VA's method. Additionally, while many noted that they had heard of many of the tools, quite a few mentioned that they had never actually applied them; thus, the practical exercises during the training were valuable to participants. Team members from the state seemed especially appreciative of learning specifics about the tools because it gave them a better understanding of and appreciation for the work that hospitals and other providers often go through to investigate a patient safety issue.

For the most part, team members interviewed—especially those from hospitals—had some experience with developing patient safety-related interventions. However, many underscored that the interventions often had more of a general quality-improvement focus, not patient safety per se (e.g., administering medications as called for in evidence-based practice guidelines, as opposed to preventing wrong medication dosage due to communication errors). Team members did have some experience with conducting evaluations of intervention programs, but many felt their evaluations had not been very sophisticated methodologically. Additionally, most noted that, although their general quality-improvement–evaluation experience was substantial, their experience evaluating patient safety programs was not, especially not on a large scale.

While the PSIC training did not result in the creation of many reporting systems (many already existed), it did affect improvements in existing ones. Several of the 11 states interviewed either already had had a medical-error–reporting system in place for several years or had recently implemented one. Some of these states noted that the PSIC training helped them to rethink their system, assess strengths and weaknesses, and make changes. At least one state underscored that the information gained through the PSIC provided the legitimacy, momentum, and feedback needed to make changes that might never have occurred or that would have taken place at a much slower pace.

Content of the PSIC Training

- *Key points:* The Year 1 PSIC participants generally felt that the training content was targeted at the appropriate level. RCA and HFMEA were the tools most often used in their jobs. The teams undertook a wide variation in team-project topics, and trainees considered that most projects had been successful. However, they encountered some barriers and noted that work remained to be done after completing the training. To improve the program content, the trainees suggested more hands-on exercises, more direction about practical interventions, and more time for discussion.

Most teams felt that the level of information provided during the training and in the homework assignments was appropriate. However, some teams noted that if their knowledge of patient safety skills and tools had been more limited at the outset, they would have had a hard time following the presentations. Several also noted that the techniques taught sometimes were too detailed and too time-consuming for their practical purposes (e.g., probabilistic risk assessment or "PRA"). However, most valued learning these tools and had incorporated at least some aspects of them into their operations at home, which is consistent with the guidance given to them by the VA to apply and adapt the tools to fit their unique operating situations. Time was the biggest challenge that teams mentioned in terms of getting their PSIC work done, given that they were juggling the PSIC training with their normal professional responsibilities.

RCA and HFMEA were the two tools most often used by teams back in their current jobs; human factors and patient safety culture training was also valued. Many teams reported that they were sharing materials and concepts with colleagues at their organizations. Most indicated that, by the end of the PSIC training, they felt that they had the skills to select an appropriate tool to investigate an error, conduct an investigation, prepare a report, develop an intervention, measure and evaluate the intervention, and translate that intervention into standard clinical practice. However, some would have liked more exercises to boost their confidence levels in their ability to teach or explain the specifics to others at their institutions, as well as more direction about the most successful types of interventions (e.g., examples, improvements possible to implement at different junctures in the rollout).

While participants were generally pleased with the course content, they offered some suggestions for improvements. Teams voiced an interest in the following:

- more case studies and group discussions so that they could learn from others' experiences
- an overview of patient safety activities in each state
- more information on fatigue and patient safety, as well as on strategies to change harmful clinical work environments
- direction on how to train others in the skills and tools learned through the PSIC (thus revealing interest in the train-the-trainer model that AHRQ has envisioned as the next step for the PSIC)
- suggestions for how regulatory agencies and providers can work together more collaboratively
- shorter presentations about each state team's project, to leave more time for discussion.

The focus of Year 1 team projects varied. Many were analytic in nature and used RCAs or HFMEAs, reflecting the request that teams focus on these two methods in their projects; others assessed a given area of concern and sometimes made related improvements. For example, in response to a new state law, the Minnesota team addressed patient safety culture by targeting organization-specific and broader environmental factors. A central part of their project was the designing and hosting of a "Just Culture Summit" of stakeholders in the state. The summit included both lectures and interactive sessions. In another example, the Alaska team focused on the process of transferring a patient from facility to facility. Alaska team members conducted an HFMEA to identify problematic steps in the transfer process, narrowed their focus to preparing documentation on medication, and worked with a collaborative to standardize documentation of transfers. Table 2.1 presents the projects carried out by the Year 1 PSIC trainee teams.

Most teams felt that they had been successful in carrying out their projects and had accomplished a significant amount. However, many did not consider their projects "complete" at the close of the PSIC training. Most said that their work was an ongoing process that would need to continue after the end of the training to be meaningful and reap full benefits. In that vein, some teams had already started to train others at their institutions about the skills and tools needed to keep their projects going. A few teams were disappointed that they were not able to make all the changes originally envisioned—especially if the team's ambition had been a statewide launch of a patient safety intervention. Some were discouraged that, although they worked hard, they were nowhere near solving their patient safety problem at the end of the PSIC training.

Table 2.1
Team Projects of Year 1 PSIC Trainees

State	Project Title
Alaska	Analyzing the Process of Transferring a Patient from Facility to Facility
Connecticut	Improvement of Adverse Event Reporting to the Department of Public Health
Maryland	Developing a Root Cause Analysis Evaluation Tool
Massachusetts	Application of Healthcare Failure Mode Effect Analysis to the Management of the Neurological Patient Population in a Rehabilitation Hospital Setting to Reduce Falls and Injury
Minnesota	Creating a Just Culture—Lessons Learned for Minnesota
Missouri	Collaborative Learning About Safety Surveillance Data
New York	New York Patient Occurrence and Tracking System (NYPORTS) Patient Safety Initiative
North Carolina	HFMEA on the Process Used to Prevent Pressure Ulcers
Oregon	Using Adverse Event Data—Survey of Oregon Hospitals
Pennsylvania	Creating a Culture of Safety
Rhode Island	The "Rhode" to Patient Safety—Improving the Reporting of "Close Call" Events
Texas	Texas Patient Safety Improvement Corps Team
Utah	Utah Patient Safety Collaborative Improvement Project—Detection, Assessment, and Intervention
Virginia	Introducing New Tools into an Established Patient Safety Program
Wisconsin	Two related projects: (1) Neuroscience Unit Fall Reduction, and (2) An Aggregate Root Cause Analysis of Falls Within a Four-Hospital Safety Collaboration (Madison Patient Safety Collaborative)

NOTE: Year 1 trainees participated in the 2003–2004 training round.

Teams mentioned many challenges to reaching their project's goals. For the most part, teams were able to devise ways of overcoming these challenges, but in some cases a solution was not readily apparent. Table 2.2 outlines the most frequently mentioned challenges, gives examples of each, and notes how the team(s) tried to overcome them (if possible) and their suggestions for addressing these challenges.

Short-Term Impact of the PSIC Training

- *Key points*: Trainees used the skills and tools taught through the PSIC in real time as the training progressed and shared them with others throughout the course of the program, especially the RCAs, HFMEAs, and reporting systems. By the third and final week of their training, many Year 1 trainees were planning or implementing initiatives in a variety of areas, although they noted significant barriers to progress. Participants had gained increased confidence and a more in-depth appreciation of the complexities of patient safety, but they underscored a need for continued training beyond the end of the PSIC program.

Participants in the PSIC training reported using many of the skills they learned and materials provided during training. The materials in the PSIC binder and the books were mentioned as being particularly helpful, and participants said that they had actively shared them with others. Almost all teams had conducted an RCA, although some noted that they used a modified version because the VA's technique was "too cumbersome" or "involved" for everyday use in busy clinical settings. To a lesser extent, many had also conducted HFMEAs. Additionally, some state team members reported using the training to inform state reporting systems and patient safety legislation, and to educate state surveyors.

Teams had implemented or were planning to implement a variety of initiatives as a result of the PSIC training. Some examples are as follows:

- enhancements to the state reporting system
- training of staff regarding correct surgical site
- training of patients to reduce risks associated with high-alert medications
- interventions to reduce falls
- programs to enhance communication at critical junctures (e.g., prescription and blood bank orders)
- usability testing of equipment, especially during the purchasing process
- courses to teach medical residents about patient safety
- methods of making adverse event reporting useful but less cumbersome for hospitals.

Table 2.2

Challenges Experienced by Year 1 (2003–2004) PSIC Trainees While Conducting Their PSIC Projects

Challenges	Examples of Challenges	Ways Teams Addressed Challenges or Suggested They Be Addressed in the Future
Distrust (hospitals/front-line caregivers vs. state regulators)	Hospital staff not wanting to report errors out of fear of repercussions	Created a "firewall" between state and hospital; tried to get all players to talk and understand the other perspective
Lack of patient safety culture	Hospital staff unable or unwilling to acknowledge patient safety problem(s)	Showed actual data to skeptics; trained hospital-based champions of patient safety
Lack of full support for PSIC involvement from supervisor or CEO	Supervisor or CEO complaining of PSIC time commitment (e.g., time out of office, team project)	No solution(s) mentioned; AHRQ anticipated the need for CEO support with letters of commitment, but competing work needs can create tensions
Lack of resources for patient safety–related actions (both PSIC-related and more general patient safety)	No staff with analytic capabilities; PSIC work piled on top of normal job responsibilities; no flexible funding to provide clinicians with non-clinic hours to participate in RCAs	No solution(s) mentioned for this barrier
Steep learning curve of those at home institutions not on PSIC team	Staff at home institutions did not know how to conduct an RCA	Suggestion: Educate staff at home institutions (possible but very time-consuming)
Geographic distance from PSIC team members	Team members too far away from each other to have regular face-to-face meetings	Held frequent telephone meetings and used email
Lack of commitment of all PSIC team members	Some team members were "free riders" (i.e., doing minimal project work)	Suggestion: Require PSIC participants to sign a formal document outlining the required commitment to the team project and time involved
Lack of state support	Could not expand PSIC project beyond team institutions because the state would not cooperate in and/or lend resources to fund expansion plans	Suggestion: Require states to sign a document that they will actively participate in the PSIC project design and will support implementation efforts statewide
Inadequate data on patient safety issues	Missing key variables related to adverse events	Added data to patient safety database from already-available data sources that were not being utilized, such as from death certificates; changed expectations to be more realistic, given data limitations
Lack of sustainability of project	No funding to continue project after PSIC training ends	No solution(s) mentioned for this barrier

After the training, participants generally felt confident in their ability to use the PSIC skills and tools, and most stated that they would do so, especially those skills related to RCA and patient safety culture. State team members in particular noted that the PSIC training gave them a greater understanding of the complexity of assessing medical errors and of the challenges involved in improving patient safety in hospitals. However, the following barriers were noted:

- fear of punishment by regulatory agencies upon identification of a problem
- unrealistic and burdensome reporting requirements (especially for less-serious adverse events)
- time limitations of clinicians to participate in RCAs and HFMEAs
- lack of time and adequate skill to educate those who had not attended the PSIC training
- lack of understanding and support of senior management regarding the reasons for errors (i.e., culture of blaming the individual, rather than looking at system deficiencies)
- lack of data regarding the return on investment ("ROI") for patient safety efforts.

With regard to their comfort level in analyzing data, comments were mixed coming out of the third and final week of the PSIC training. Some trainees (especially those with quantitative backgrounds) felt confident, whereas others noted continued weaknesses in this regard. Many trainees expressed concern about the lack of trustworthy, available data to track medical errors and adverse events.

Many teams noted that one or more hospitals in their states had assessed patient safety culture using a survey. However, such assessments did not appear to be widespread in most states at that time. When surveys had been conducted at multiple hospitals in a state, trainees reported that there was wide variation in patient safety culture and few incentives to report medical errors.

When asked about the types of initiatives they could imagine launching in hospitals around their states to improve patient safety, trainees made several suggestions, including the following:

- forming a state collaborative or patient safety center to hold annual conferences so that more could benefit from the experiences of individual institutions
- establishing less burdensome requirements for reporting medical errors
- streamlining reporting documents so that they are less cumbersome to fill out
- training consumers to be more active partners in patient safety
- launching more widespread training of sharp-end clinicians—especially as part of medical and nursing school curricula and/or other educational programs geared to clinicians at teaching hospitals
- requiring any institution that receives state funding to do a culture survey and teach courses on best patient safety practices to staff
- conducting educational courses about coding medical errors
- educating staff at all levels about moving from a culture of blame to a culture of support that focuses on eliminating system-level threats to patient safety.

Finally, PSIC trainees offered some suggestions regarding resources that would facilitate their ability to use the patient safety methods and tools taught through the PSIC. Most trainees felt that they needed more guidance about becoming effective trainers and prioritizing their next steps—needs AHRQ anticipated early on and aimed to address with the train-the-trainer program. The majority also voiced an interest in continuing educational opportunities through the PSIC after the official end of the training—including continued contact with AHRQ, the VA NCPS, PSIC faculty, and other PSIC teams. Some noted concern about lack of funds to continue implementation of their PSIC project and to launch new projects, as well as about the lack of training available for the leadership in their institutions to learn about the importance of patient safety.

FEEDBACK ON THE PSIC EXPERIENCE ONE YEAR LATER

From March through May 2005, a team of RAND researchers conducted telephone interviews with representatives from each state team that participated in the Year 1 PSIC training. Our goal was to interview one individual from each participating organization on each state team. We achieved this goal for all but three states. In each of these three states, we were unable to interview a representative from one organization on the team. In all, we interviewed 38 individuals (15 representing the state and 23 representing hospitals)[1] from the 15 participating state teams to

- Learn about their use and application of the PSIC skills and tools during the year following the last training session.
- Solicit feedback for improving the program, given hindsight of one year.

Interviewers used a structured protocol comprising both open-ended and close-ended questions (see Appendix B); interviews lasted approximately one hour. The findings from these interviews are summarized below.

Attendance and Support Needed to Attend PSIC Training

- *Key points*: Attendance at all the Year 1, week-long training sessions was consistent and strong. The majority of participants felt that they received adequate support from their home institutions to attend the training and carry out the team project. However, they also mentioned that the time to do reading assignments and team project work was often an "add on," above and beyond their normal workloads. Trainees encouraged any organization contemplating participation in the PSIC to be receptive to the knowledge that participants bring from the course and to realize the intensity of the commitment of staff time for the PSIC training.

Attendance across the three Year 1 training sessions was strong. Of the 38 individuals interviewed, 33 (87 percent) were able to participate in all three week-long courses. The five individuals who were not able to attend the training program in its entirety cited illness or conflicts at work beyond their control (e.g., a governor's meeting).

---

[1]   Of the 38 organizations interviewed, three entities were initially coded as "other" in terms of organization type. However, during the course of our interviews, it made sense to recode them as either "state" or "hospital" due to the nature of their organization (provider or regulator) and the role they played on their state team.

Overall, 34 (89 percent) of the 38 PSIC participants we interviewed—both hospital and state representatives—felt that their organizations gave them adequate support to fully participate in the training and complete the team project. (We note that this organizational support differs from the issue raised by some participants of inadequate CEO support for the teams in conducting their PSIC project, which involves a higher level of commitment than sending them for training. We also note that CEOs of organizations sending an employee to the PSIC were required to sign a commitment letter, and to participate in a telephone call to learn about their employee(s)' participation in the PSIC and its impact on their organization. Many noted that patient safety is an integral part of their jobs, so participation was viewed as an important professional learning opportunity. Many particularly voiced appreciation that AHRQ covered travel expenses and that the VA assisted with travel logistics in a timely and clear manner.

Although trainees felt supported, more than one-third of those interviewed (37 percent) also noted barriers they had to overcome to attend or fully engage in the program. For example, although their supervisors and organizations were supportive and gave them permission to be away from the office, normal work responsibilities did not vanish (they were just delayed); thus, a significant amount of catch-up was required upon return to work. Additionally, reading and homework assignments were often completed on trainees' own time (i.e., evenings, weekends). To address this issue, some suggested that having the reading list ahead of time for the entire year-long program would have been helpful to get a head start on the reading. Given these barriers, some felt that three-day training sessions would have been sufficient, especially when factoring in significant out-of-the office travel time for some trainees. In response to this feedback from the first year, AHRQ and the VA tried fewer, longer days in each session in the second year, but this configuration was not well received by participants either. The only other option would be to cut content, which would weaken the training and so was not done.

As to state team projects, some said their team could have used more detailed consultation at the first session from AHRQ and the VA to identify project topics, modify them into ones that could realistically be completed during the training year (i.e., a "reality check"), and/or outline a practical execution plan. These individuals felt they lost valuable time up front because they did not focus early enough on a topic and/or did not have a realistic plan in place for getting it done during the training year, making them feel rushed and overloaded towards the end. We note that all PSIC teams were required to propose up to two potential projects as part of their application, and were allowed to change the focus, but had to finalize their choice by the end of the second week of training. In order to make the team project component of the course more readily meaningful, it was the goal of AHRQ and the VA not to force project topics onto teams, but rather to allow teams to select topics of immediate importance to them and devise their own implementation plans given their first-hand knowledge of their own organizations. Finally, several state employees noted that it was extremely difficult to be away from their states during key legislative periods, but they understood that it is hard for PSIC planners to work around such schedules, given that each state's schedule is different.

Those we interviewed offered some thoughts and advice to other organizations that might be interested in sending staff to the PSIC training, about the level of support they should realistically expect to provide:

- Above all, trainees emphasized the importance of having support from all levels of the sponsoring organization, not only by sending staff to the training but also by embracing the knowledge that participants bring back to the organization. The organization should be interested in what was learned, encourage staff to share what they learned with others, and be committed to patient safety for the long term.

- Trainees repeatedly underscored the time commitment involved in having staff be part of the year-long PSIC program. Organizations must realize that employees will be out of the office for a total of three weeks, during which they will not have time to do any other work. Additionally, travel time to and from the training sites must be factored in, as must the time it takes to do the homework and, especially, the team project. The team project may also involve additional travel if team members live far apart and need to meet in person. In other words, participation should not be viewed solely as three weeks out of the office; a significant time commitment beyond that is involved if the organization really wants to reap the full benefits of the training. Many teams also noted the importance of team continuity; as such, organizations must be willing to send the same person to all sessions. Given the significant time commitment, several trainees advised that organizations reassign work wherever possible to give the PSIC trainee time to focus on the training. (We note again that time at work was an anticipated issue and a letter of commitment from CEOs in support of their employees' participation in the PSIC was a requisite of the PSIC application.)

- Regarding the team project, PSIC participants advised team members to get early buy-in from their organizations for their proposed topic so as not to meet with resistance later; organizations should be engaged in the project topic and, it is hoped, willing to see it through past the end of the PSIC training.

Despite the caveats noted, especially the recognition of the significant time investment, the overwhelming majority of trainees voiced strong support for attendance, saying it was "a great investment" and "absolutely worth it."

Usefulness of the PSIC Tools in Actual Practice One Year Later

- *Key points*: One year after their PSIC training ended, the Year 1 participants reported that the training had been most useful to them in learning about RCA, HFMEA, human factors engineering, and the reporting of adverse events and near misses. Hospital representatives most often reported using the tools and skills related to RCA, human factors engineering, and reporting of adverse events and near misses. State representatives said that they regularly used the human factors engineering and reporting of adverse events tools and skills. Trainees valued the consultative services of the VA and AHRQ, as well as the extensive library provided to each PSIC participant.

- Additionally, participants viewed the networking opportunities and first-hand experience of hospitals and states working collaboratively on patient safety issues as PSIC tools and skills that are equally as important as didactic learning and reading materials. They would have liked to have more training and hands-on exercises, as well as refresher courses and literature updates, to help them retain knowledge on the cutting edge of patient safety science.

We asked the Year 1 trainees a series of questions about specific tools and skills taught during the PSIC training. In particular, we wanted to determine whether—with the perspective of one year post training—the trainees thought that it had been useful overall to learn about the given skill or tool, as well as whether they actually use each skill or tool in everyday practice. We present here the trainees' assessments for each of the 12 tools we discussed with them in the interviews. We report separately the feedback by the state and hospital participants, recognizing their distinct, and often complementary, needs and priorities. As shown in our findings, the inclusion of the hospitals' representatives in the training, as requested by the state participants, has expanded both the scope of knowledge and practices in the field across both types of organizations.

Detailed responses to this series of questions on the value and use of the PSIC skills and tools are presented in Table 2.3. Responses are given for the overall group of trainees and by organization type (i.e., states and hospitals). Of note, many who said they were not using the PSIC skills or tools remarked that no help is needed to do so; the skills and tools simply were not applicable in the context of their current jobs.

Root Cause Analysis (RCA): Almost all of the state and hospital representatives with whom we spoke (93 percent and 96 percent, respectively) said that, overall, it was useful to learn about RCA. Both groups felt that learning about RCA in the PSIC training helped them put a more concrete structure around a process with which many were already familiar. They also found the practice exercises during the training informative. However, a greater proportion of hospitals (87 percent) than states (67 percent) said they actually use RCAs in practice. State regulators tend to use their knowledge of RCA gained through the PSIC training to establish standards of reporting and to educate their own staff (e.g., investigators, prosecutors of medical error cases) about the complex array of factors that impact the provision of medical care in the U.S. health care system. These regulators often noted that learning about RCA helped them to appreciate that medical errors often arise due to system—not individual—deficiencies; it also made them realize that there is a need for the judicial system to reevaluate its tendency to search for an individual to blame when a medical error occurs.

Most commonly, hospitals reported using their knowledge of RCA to investigate sentinel events or near misses. Other instances in which hospitals use the RCA information include training trainers within their organization or state, educating medical and nursing students, and coupling RCA information with human factors information to better understand causes of error. Many hospital representatives voiced appreciation for the rigorous RCA methods, although some thought that those methods were too time-consuming and staff-intensive for them to be able to use. Therefore, many said they are using a simpler, modified version. (We note that during the training, the VA instructor advises participants to use what is best for them while encouraging them to use the full method.)

Those who did not tend to use RCA in practice said that performing such analyses was not a function of their organization or part of their specific job responsibilities. However, many remarked that, although they may not perform RCAs often or ever, they frequently drew upon the RCA-related concepts they learned.

Healthcare Failure Mode and Effects Analysis (HFMEA): As with RCA, a very high proportion of participants from both states and hospitals interviewed (93 percent and 96 percent, respectively) found it useful to learn about HFMEA, especially the comprehensive approach advocated by the VA. Also similar to RCA, a higher proportion of hospital participants (65 percent) than state participants (47 percent) use HFMEA in practice. Those who use HFMEA tend to employ the concepts to better understand possible pitfalls before implementing a new practice or technology or before making substantial changes. Some noted that the PSIC training on this topic helped them guide ongoing research at their organizations and that this topic area was particularly useful, given JCAHO's requirement for hospitals to do at least one FMEA per year.

Several of those who indicated that it was not useful to learn about HFMEA at the PSIC training said that they had already learned about it prior to the course. Some of those not using HFMEA on a regular basis noted that they were interested in doing so but had not yet had the opportunity. Others said that, while they do not use it because they do not operate in a clinical setting, they frequently teach the concepts to others. Quite a few underscored that they do not use HFMEA often or at all because it is hard for them to get buy-in to do so; HFMEA is often seen by front-line staff as involving too much conjecture, being too tedious and cumbersome a process, and lacking in both structure and focus. Smaller facilities with limited staff especially seem to have difficulty using this technique.

Probabilistic Risk Assessment (PRA): Despite the fact that almost two-thirds of the participants we interviewed (60 percent of states and 65 percent of hospitals) said it was helpful to learn about PRA, only 13 percent of each organization type reported using this tool with any regularity. Of note, many of those who said they use PRA do so only in the context of conducting an HFMEA. The following reasons were given for not using PRA:

- The tool is too complex and statistical for use by beginners, especially after only a cursory introduction in one PSIC training session.

- The PSIC session was not taught well and began at too high a level for the audience.

- The need to purchase software before being able to use this analytic method is a significant impediment.

- The technique is too theoretical for practicing clinical staff.

We note that the team participants were critical of the PRA training in the first year. The course and instructor were changed for the second year, with more favorable feedback from the participants on the revised approach. However, some participants continued to express concerns about the complexity of the PRA methods and feasibility for them to use it.

VA's Safety Assessment Code (SAC): A large proportion of state and hospital representatives interviewed (80 percent and 87 percent, respectively) found it useful to learn about the VA's SAC, and a reasonably high proportion of each (33 percent of states and 48 percent of hospitals) said they use this tool in practice. Many organizations that use it have incorporated it into their RCA process as a way to determine when to conduct an RCA, especially for near misses, for which the investment of time to do an RCA may not be as compelling as in cases of actual adverse events. Some of those not using the VA's SAC noted that they were already using another, similar tool prior to the PSIC training and did not change to the VA's method because staff is used to their current method.

Human factors engineering: Human factors engineering was a well-received topic, with 93 percent of responding state staff and 91 percent of responding hospital staff saying they appreciated learning about it. It is also a tool both states and hospitals use in practice (i.e., 53 percent of state representatives and 83 percent of hospital representatives). Those who use it noted that they incorporate it into their RCA process, use it to inform equipment purchases, and refer to it frequently in educational sessions about patient safety (e.g., showing new clinicians the pitfalls of current equipment). Many also commented that the human factors engineering perspective is a valuable way of looking at every medical error and at every opportunity for a medical error; "it's a new way of thinking that informs my job," remarked one trainee. Those not using this tool in practice typically said it was out of the scope of their job, but a useful concept to have learned.

Patient safety culture survey and tools: Approximately half of responding states (53 percent) and three-quarters (74 percent) of responding hospital staff said they thought it was informative to learn about patient safety culture surveys and related tools. Not surprisingly, given the direct application to clinical settings, more hospital staff (39 percent) reported actually using such tools than did state staff (13 percent). Hospital staff said that it was often eye-opening to conduct a culture survey, given that results did not always match staff expectations. These tools are also viewed as a good way to identify weaknesses to target for improvement. Some reasons offered for not fielding surveys were lack of resources to do so or current use of culture tools other than those presented at the PSIC. The need for a nationally accepted, standard survey was expressed. One individual remarked that current culture tools are too hospital-specific and need to be expanded to reflect other settings (e.g., outpatient clinics, long-term care). Finally, several participants noted that they found the presentation on just culture helpful.

AHRQ's Patient Safety Indicators (PSIs):[2] Proportionately more state staff than hospital staff (80 percent and 61 percent, respectively) found AHRQ's PSIs useful to learn about. However, a greater proportion of hospital staff than state staff said they actually use the PSIs in everyday practice (52 percent and 27 percent, respectively). Most of the hospital staff who reported using the PSIs said that such use was not a direct result of the PSIC training, because they were already using them before the training; but many indicated that the training helped them appreciate these indicators more and exposed them to new ways to use, organize, and report them. Several hospital staff noted that there is an urgent need to validate these measures to make them more credible, and encouraged AHRQ to do so. At least one hospital participant underscored that there are known limitations of the data used to score PSIs, limitations that lead to the skepticism about these indicators. Some of the limitations mentioned include variations in coding practices in different locales, as well as across the country, and limitations regarding the number of codes captured. State representatives not using the PSIs typically said that using them was not within the scope of their jobs.

Tools to identify high-alert medications: Participants from states and hospitals thought it was helpful to learn about tools to identify high-alert medications (80 percent and 65 percent, respectively). A smaller proportion of hospital staff than state staff said they were actually using these tools in the daily aspects of their work (43 percent and 60 percent, respectively). Feelings were mixed about the actual training session on this topic: Some considered it far too technical,

---

2 The AHRQ Patient Safety Indicators (PSIs) were developed by the Evidence-Based Practice Center at the University of California, San Diego; Stanford University; and the University of California, Davis, using the Healthcare Cost and Utilization Project (HCUP) Nationwide Inpatient Sample (NIS) of hospital discharges. The PSIs capture events in hospital inpatient services, focusing on in-hospital complications and adverse events following surgeries, procedures, and childbirth (McDonald, Romano, Geppert, et al., (2002).

especially for a "non-pharmaceutical group"; others found the presentation excellent. Of note, many organizations that said they were using these tools also noted that they had had a focus on high-alert medications before the PSIC training (i.e., their use of these tools was not entirely due to the PSIC). States in particular found this information useful to draw upon during investigations and site visits. Additionally, many who said they were not using the PSIC tools in their daily practice noted that they are using other tools to address this issue, that they have shared the PSIC materials on this topic with others, and/or that this topic area was not in the purview of their job (i.e., it was already being handled by staff in the pharmacy department).

Analysis of patient safety data: Training about how to analyze patient safety data seemed to be both more appreciated and more used by participants from states than by those from hospitals. While nearly three-quarters (73 percent) of the state staff we interviewed found this topic useful to learn about and 60 percent said they use the information in daily practice, only 43 percent of hospital staff found the topic useful and only 30 percent actually use the information on a regular basis. State representatives said this topic was relevant to their evaluation of adverse event reports, RCAs, and HFMEAs. Some hospital staff pointed out that they already have analytic units that conduct such analyses, so the PSIC training did not add much to their institutional knowledge in this regard and/or they are interested in the topic but "just haven't gotten to it" yet. Several participants, from both states and hospitals, remarked that they could not remember this part of the PSIC training very well, if at all.

Reporting of adverse events and near misses: The PSIC training related to the reporting of adverse events and near misses was very well received and well used by participants from both states and hospitals. All state staff and 87 percent of hospital staff we interviewed appreciated the training on this subject matter, and a high proportion of both said they use the information regularly (80 percent and 78 percent, respectively). Those with positive comments about this training noted the following benefits: It helped them learn how to identify trends and categorize data, was related to recently passed legislation and/or helped inform proposed laws, was useful to support proposals for the acquisition of online reporting systems and to inform purchasing decisions, and encouraged their institutions to focus on near misses in addition to adverse events. Many participants pointed out that they were already involved in this area prior to the PSIC, but they said they still found the training to be useful because it provided reassurance that the organization was "on the right track." Those who did not find this part of the training useful or do not regularly draw upon it typically said either that this area was not a part of their job or that they already had a system in place that was working well prior to the PSIC.

Tools to assess the business case for patient safety: A greater proportion of hospital staff than state staff found it useful to learn about tools to assess the business case for patient safety. More than three-quarters (78 percent) of the hospital staff we interviewed thought this material was informative, whereas about half (53 percent) of those from the states did. Hospital participants also tended to report using this information more regularly than those from the states (26 percent of hospitals versus only 7 percent of states). Hospital representatives not using these tools often cited the following reasons: lack of time and budget, limited or no access to data, and no need because the organization is committed to patient safety no matter the cost. Many state representatives not using these tools said they were not relevant professionally; however, some said that they had shared the information with others. Others felt they were not qualified to run such analyses, even after the PSIC training.

Tools to evaluate patient safety programs: More than two-thirds (67 percent) of state participants, compared with less than half (43 percent) of hospital participants, found the PSIC training about evaluating patient safety programs to be informative. Many, especially hospital representatives, remarked that they did not recall this part of the training or felt that it had not been very thorough. A greater proportion of state staff than hospital staff (27 percent versus 17 percent) said they actually use this information in practice. Many of those not using this information regularly said that they had not yet had time, but hoped to. At least one state representative felt the context of an evaluation provided a good opportunity to raise issues of patient safety culture with her staff.

Additional comments on tools: Many of those interviewed provided additional comments about the skills and tools taught during the PSIC training. A number of trainees underscored that the opportunity to network during the training was equally as important as the skills and tools they were taught. Many viewed their contacts coming out of the PSIC training as valuable tools they have drawn upon frequently. (The initial enthusiasm appears to wane with time, according to our follow-up interview findings, which showed that only about 40 percent of graduates remained in contact after the training ended, as reported below.) Additionally, some noted that learning how to convince normally adversarial entities to talk about patient safety issues together and using the same language to do so were very important skills acquired during the training.

Trainees also emphasized the usefulness of the hands-on exercises, no matter the tool or skill being taught. They felt it was important to learn about a topic and then be able to apply it immediately to understand its use in the real world. At least one trainee found the training related to educating residents and fellows about patient safety useful. The AHRQ and VA Web sites were also mentioned as useful tools, especially the AHRQ Morbidity and Mortality Web site (WebM&M) (http://webmm.ahrq.gov).

As to criticisms, at least one trainee noted that many of the tools were geared to hospitals and hoped that future training would include courses on helping health departments and other state entities understand how they can use the PSIC skills and tools. Some, especially those from hospitals, found it odd that the training attempted to separate patient safety from other quality of care concerns, given that these two areas overlap considerably (e.g., ventilator-related pneumonia can be viewed as both a safety concern and a quality concern).

We also asked Year 1 trainees what help, if any, they need to use the skills and tools they do not currently use but would like to. Trainees thought that AHRQ or the VA could assist with the following:

- more exposure to real-world examples and hands-on training
- additional training regarding PRA, RCA, and the business case for safety
- regional lectures by AHRQ and VA staff to help educate individuals who did not attend the PSIC training
- occasional reminders about available tools, as well as when and why to use them, given that trainees say it is easy to forget this information post training
- reference lists from the medical literature that support patient safety interventions, so that trainees can provide skeptics with this documentation

- advice regarding the use of PSIs for reporting, given that such use is occurring despite AHRQ's recommendation to the contrary
- validation of AHRQ's PSIs to lend credibility
- periodic refresher courses.

Trainees also noted that they need the following in order to use the PSIC skills and tools, but did not think AHRQ or the VA could help in these areas:

- securing buy-in from board members or other managers to make patient safety a priority
- overcoming the resistance of colleagues to change their current behavior
- more resources at their home institutions (e.g., money, staff, time).

Resources or Support for Trainee Activities

Several hospital representatives remarked that one pleasant outcome of the PSIC is that they view their state colleagues as a resource for help, rather than as an adversary, and have contacted them for assistance. PSIC participants reported that they call upon many different resources when they need help, including, most frequently,

- consulting the PSIC training manuals, handouts, or library
- contacting their own team members or other state teams
- contacting the PSIC VA staff and others at the NCPS
- referring to information posted on AHRQ's or the VA's Web sites
- contacting PSIC instructors directly
- participating in conference calls sponsored by the VA.

Table 2.3
Follow-Up Interview Responses for Year 1 PSIC Trainees on the Usefulness
of the Skills and Tools Taught During the PSIC Training

Tool or Skill	Useful Overall?	Actually Use in Practice?
Root Cause Analysis		
Total		
Yes	95% (36/38)	79% (30/38)
No	0% (0/38)	21% (8/38)
NA	5% (2/38)	0% (0/38)
State		
Yes	93% (14/15)	67% (10/15)
No	0% (0/15)	33% (5/15)
NA	7% (1/15)	0% (0/15)
Hospital		
Yes	96% (22/23)	87% (20/23)
No	0% (0/23)	13% (3/23)
NA	4% (1/23)	0% (0/23)
Healthcare Failure Mode and Effects		
Analysis		
Total		
Yes	95% (36/38)	58% (22/38)
No	0% (0/38)	42% (16/38)
NA	5% (2/38)	0% (0/38)
State		
Yes	93% (14/15)	47% (7/15)
No	0% (0/15)	53% (8/15)
NA	7% (1/15)	0% (0/15)
Hospital		
Yes	96% (22/23)	65% (15/23)
No	0% (0/23)	35% (8/23)
NA	4% (1/23)	0% (0/23)
Probabilistic risk assessment		
Total		
Yes	63% (24/38)	13% (5/38)
No	29% (11/38)	84% (32/38)
NA	8% (3/38)	3% (1/38)
State		
Yes	60% (9/15)	13% (2/15)
No	33% (5/15)	87% (13/15)
NA	7% (1/15)	0% (0/15)
Hospital		
Yes	65% (15/23)	13% (3/23)
No	26% (6/23)	83% (19/23)
NA	9% (2/23)	4% (1/23)

Table 2.3—Continued

Tool or Skill	Useful Overall?	Actually Use in Practice?
VA's Safety Assessment Code		
Total		
Yes	84% (32/38)	42% (16/38)
No	8% (3/38)	55% (21/38)
NA	8% (3/38)	3% (1/38)
State		
Yes	80% (12/15)	33% (5/15)
No	13% (2/15)	67% (10/15)
NA	7% (1/15)	0% (0/15)
Hospital		
Yes	87% (20/23)	48% (11/23)
No	4% (1/23)	48% (11/23)
NA	9% (2/23)	4% (1/23)
Human factors engineering		
Total		
Yes	92% (35/38)	71% (27/38)
No	5% (2/38)	29% (11/38)
NA	3% (1/38)	0% (0/38)
State		
Yes	93% (14/15)	53% (8/15)
No	0% (0/15)	47% (7/15)
NA	7% (1/15)	0% (0/15)
Hospital		
Yes	91% (21/23)	83% (19/23)
No	9% (2/23)	17% (4/23)
NA	0% (0/23)	0% (0/23)
Patient safety culture survey and tools		
Total		
Yes	66% (25/38)	29% (11/38)
No	21% (8/38)	61% (23/38)
Yes/No	3% (1/38)	3% (1/38)
NA	11% (4/38)	8% (3/38)
State		
Yes	53% (8/15)	13% (2/15)
No	27% (4/15)	67% (10/15)
Yes/No	0% (0/15)	0% (0/15)
NA	20% (3/15)	20% (3/15)
Hospital		
Yes	74% (17/23)	39% (9/23)
No	17% (4/23)	57% (13/23)
Yes/No	4% (1/23)	4% (1/23)
NA	4% (1/23)	0% (0/23)

Table 2.3—Continued

Tool or Skill	Useful Overall?	Actually Use in Practice?
Patient safety indicators		
Total		
Yes	68% (26/38)	42% (16/38)
No	18% (7/38)	55% (21/38)
Yes/No	3% (1/38)	0% (0/38)
NA	11% (4/38)	3% (1/38)
State		
Yes	80% (12/15)	27% (4/15)
No	13% (2/15)	73% (11/15)
Yes/No	0% (0/15)	0% (0/15)
NA	7% (1/15)	0% (0/15)
Hospital		
Yes	61% (14/23)	52% (12/23)
No	22% (5/23)	43% (10/23)
Yes/No	4% (1/23)	0% (0/23)
NA	13% (3/23)	4% (1/23)
Tools to identify high-alert medications		
Total		
Yes	71% (27/38)	50% (19/38)
No	16% (6/38)	42% (16/38)
NA	13% (5/38)	8% (3/38)
State		
Yes	80% (12/15)	60% (9/15)
No	7% (1/15)	33% (5/15)
NA	13% (2/15)	7% (1/15)
Hospital		
Yes	65% (15/23)	43% (10/23)
No	22% (5/23)	48% (11/23)
NA	13% (3/23)	9% (2/23)
Analysis of patient safety data		
Total		
Yes	55% (21/38)	42% (16/38)
No	13% (5/38)	39% (15/38)
NA	32% (12/38)	18% (7/38)
State		
Yes	73% (11/15)	60% (9/15)
No	20% (3/15)	33% (5/15)
NA	7% (1/15)	7% (1/15)
Hospital		
Yes	43% (10/23)	30% (7/23)
No	9% (2/23)	43% (10/23)
NA	48% (11/23)	26% (6/23)

Table 2.3—Continued

Tool or Skill	Useful Overall?	Actually Use in Practice?
Reporting of adverse events and near misses		
Total		
Yes	92% (35/38)	79% (30/38)
No	3% (1/38)	16% (6/38)
NA	5% (2/38)	5% (2/38)
State		
Yes	100% (15/15)	80% (12/15)
No	0% (0/15)	20% (3/15)
NA	0% (0/15)	0% (0/15)
Hospital		
Yes	87% (20/23)	78% (18/23)
No	4% (1/23)	13% (3/23)
NA	9% (2/23)	9% (2/23)
Tools to assess patient safety business case		
Total		
Yes	68% (26/38)	18% (7/38)
No	18% (7/38)	66% (25/38)
NA	13% (5/38)	16% (6/38)
State		
Yes	53% (8/15)	7% (1/15)
No	33% (5/15)	67% (10/15)
NA	13% (2/15)	27% (4/15)
Hospital		
Yes	78% (18/23)	26% (6/23)
No	9% (2/23)	65% (15/23)
NA	13% (3/23)	9% (2/23)
Tools to evaluate patient safety programs		
Total		
Yes	53% (20/38)	21% (8/38)
No	13% (5/38)	42% (16/38)
NA	34% (13/38)	37% (14/38)
State		
Yes	67% (10/15)	27% (4/15)
No	27% (4/15)	53% (8/15)
NA	7% (1/15)	20% (3/15)
Hospital		
Yes	43% (10/23)	17% (4/23)
No	4% (1/23)	35% (8/23)
NA	52% (12/23)	48% (11/23)

NOTES: Year 1 trainees participated in the 2003–2004 training round.

- Percentages within a category may not sum to 100 percent due to rounding error.
- NA = Not applicable, missing, or don't know. Either not applicable per the respondent, who did not feel that the topic was relevant, given his/her specific type of organization or role within that organization; answer missing; or the respondent did not feel he/she could answer the question.
- Some respondents responded yes/no (i.e., "sort of") to some questions, but not to others. Where applicable, yes/no is listed as a response category.

When specifically asked if ongoing technical support from AHRQ or the VA would be helpful, most trainees responded yes. However, many noted that they felt such support was already provided, especially by the VA. These trainees said that they had called and emailed the VA with questions and have usually received help in a timely manner. Some remarked that AHRQ seemed too removed from the front lines to offer practical assistance in most areas, but that it could contribute substantially by validating the PSIs and providing guidance on their appropriate use. The trainees opined that the AHRQ or the VA could be of assistance in the following areas:

- online analytic support regarding the patient safety culture survey (e.g., analysis and creation of a report card)
- updates on the progress of other trainees
- access to a statistician
- updates on research, legislation in other states, and funding opportunities
- identification of credible new tools (i.e., "sorting the good stuff from the junk")
- occasional meetings to update trainees on new information
- advanced training on specific topics (e.g., PRA, RCA)
- applications to other settings (e.g., long-term care)
- continued opportunities for networking with the same class year of trainees as well as with the new classes.

Regarding the PSIC library, the trainees across the board appreciated these resources, used them regularly, and shared them with colleagues back home. Although trainees emphasized the value of having a complete library, the resources that were mentioned most frequently as being particularly useful were

- the two IOM reports (*To Err Is Human* and *Crossing the Quality Chasm)*
- *The Design of Everyday Things* by Donald Norman
- *Managing the Risks of Organizational Accidents* by James Reason
- the *Beyond Blame* video by Bridge Medical, Inc.
- the laminated instructions and examples for RCAs and HFMEAs, which are useful to train others.

IMPACT ON PATIENT SAFETY ACTIONS IN THE YEAR FOLLOWING TRAINING

- *Key points:* One year after the end of their PSIC training, both state and hospital representatives reported that the training influenced their patient safety actions in meaningful ways.

For states, the PSIC training has had the broadest effect on the initiation or revision of state regulations or legislation, on modifications to oversight procedures in the wake of an adverse event, and on modifications of an existing reporting system. To a lesser extent, states said the PSIC had facilitated the creation of a statewide reporting system, and had helped to create or improve stakeholder coalitions. For hospital representatives, the top three areas affected by the PSIC training were modification of processes to review or analyze adverse events or errors, promotion of a patient safety culture, and the sharing of data to better understand causes of error. To a lesser extent, hospital participants reported that the PSIC training facilitated other improvements in the review of adverse events or initiatives, the creation or improvement of stakeholder coalitions, and the creation of an adverse event reporting system.

We asked PSIC trainees about the effect that the training has had on patient safety–related actions. Given the different nature and goals of these two types of organizations, we asked slightly different questions of the states and the hospitals.

Actions by State Trainees

Table 2.4 summarizes our findings regarding the impact of PSIC training on practices by state representatives. Of the 15 state representatives we interviewed, nearly half (47 percent) said that the PSIC training had either helped them to initiate state regulations/legislation or had influenced the content, interpretation, and/or implementation of state regulations/legislation. For example, one state said that the PSIC training had influenced the specifications of the components of a patient safety program. The same proportion also noted that the PSIC training had contributed to the modification of hospital oversight procedures when an adverse event occurs. For example, it helped provide clearer direction regarding the information that should be included in an RCA.

Thirty-three percent noted that the PSIC training contributed to the modification of an existing state reporting system to improve how it captures patient safety issues or how information is reported to others. For example, some state representatives were trying to change the statute to make RCA information nondiscoverable.

To a lesser extent (20 percent), state representatives said that the training had facilitated the creation of a statewide reporting system; in particular, trainees noted that the training had helped them to better define the content of the reports. In many cases, the PSIC was not as influential in this regard because the state already had a statewide reporting system (i.e., established prior to the PSIC training). About one-fifth of state representatives also noted that the training had led them to either form a patient safety coalition or add new types of members to a patient safety coalition of stakeholders. For example, at least one state added a patient representative to its patient safety alliance.

Additionally, the state representatives interviewed noted some other ways in which the PSIC training had facilitated patient safety–related actions. For example, several underscored the overall improvement in the relationship between hospitals and regulators (i.e., it became more collegial than adversarial following the PSIC training), and one individual noted a commitment to eliminating the occurrence of the National Quality Forum's (NQF) 27 serious reportable events (often referred to as "never events") (NQF, 2003).

Table 2.4
Influence of PSIC Training on Patient Safety Actions by States,
Reported by Year 1 Trainees One Year Following PSIC Training

Patient Safety Action	Percentage (#) Responding "yes" (N = 15)
Initiation of or influence on regulation(s)/ legislation	47% (7)
Modification of hospital oversight procedures when an adverse event occurs (e.g., change content of Root Cause Analysis)	47 * (7)
Modification of an existing state reporting system to improve how it captures patient safety issues or how information is reported to others	33 (5)
Creation of a statewide reporting system	20 (3)
New membership in or formation of a patient safety coalition of stakeholders	20 (3)

NOTE: Year 1 trainees participated in the 2003–2004 training round.

* For 7 percent of the respondents, this question was not applicable, not relevant to the respondent's type of organization or role within that organization, or the respondent could not answer the question.

Actions by Hospital Trainees

Table 2.5 summarizes our findings regarding the effects of the Year 1 PSIC training on practices by hospitals. Of the 23 hospital representatives we interviewed, a significant majority (83 percent, or 19/23) said that the PSIC training facilitated the modification of processes to review and analyze adverse events or errors. In particular, hospital representatives noted that they added or modified their use of RCAs, HFMEAs, and human factors analysis.

More than three-quarters of the hospital representatives interviewed felt that the PSIC contributed to the promotion of a patient safety culture at their institutions. Several noted that they had conducted educational sessions or had given presentations to raise awareness about this topic as a result of their involvement in the PSIC; the target audiences varied widely from CEOs to medical and nursing students and state hospital association members.

Slightly more than half of hospital respondents thought that the PSIC facilitated sharing of data to better understand causes of error. Some felt that the PSIC had helped to bring about an "epiphany" that such sharing was a positive thing to do. Those who did not feel that the PSIC had helped in this regard noted that this was because sharing already occurred prior to the PSIC or, more frequently, that there was still significant fear about sharing such information outside their organization, especially in view of legal liability.

Table 2.5
Influence of PSIC Training on Patient Safety Actions by Hospitals,
Reported by Year 1 Trainees One Year Following PSIC Training

Patient Safety Action	Percentage Responding "yes" ($N = 23$)	
Modification of processes to review/analyze adverse events or errors	83% *	(19)
Promotion of patient safety culture	78 *	(18)
Sharing of data across organizations to better understand causes of error	52	(12)
Other changes in review of adverse events	48	(11)
Other statewide or organization wide initiatives	48 *	(11)
New membership in or formation of a patient safety group of stakeholders	35	(8)
Creation of institutional adverse event reporting system	30	(7)

NOTE: Year 1 trainees participated in the 2003–2004 training round.

* For 4 percent of the respondents, this question was not applicable, not relevant to the respondent's type of organization or role within that organization, or the respondent could not answer the question.

Approximately half said that the PSIC training had contributed to other changes in the review of adverse events (e.g., standardized process and forms, more-thorough reviews, more-consistent use of RCAs) and/or in other state- or organization-wide initiatives (e.g., programs to promote medication reconciliation or a focus on the system, not the individual, when an error occurs).

Slightly more than one-third remarked that the PSIC had facilitated new membership in or formation of a patient safety group of stakeholders. In particular, several hospital representatives said that the PSIC training had encouraged them to make such stakeholder committees more collaborative (e.g., merging the performance improvement committee with the patient safety committee) and more diverse (e.g., adding patient safety researchers, human factors engineers, and state representatives).

Almost one-third of the hospital participants reported that the PSIC training had facilitated the creation of an adverse event reporting system in their hospitals. Most who responded "no" to this question already had a system in place before the PSIC training, most likely reflecting the JCAHO requirement that hospitals have a system for reporting errors and adverse events.

In areas in which state and hospital representatives said that the PSIC training had helped to stimulate action, we asked how influential it had been. The majority of respondents said that the PSIC had been very influential, or—in the words of one trainee—"10 on a scale of 1 to 10." Some noted that their participation in the PSIC training helped to give them more confidence and more credibility upon returning to their home organizations; others said that it raised their level of sophistication about patient safety and gave them the proper structure and vocabulary. Many said that the training was the impetus for generating discussions about patient safety, for beginning to make changes, or for enhancing the quality of changes already in motion.

In areas in which trainees said that the PSIC training had not helped to stimulate action, the trainees either noted that patient safety actions were already under way prior to the PSIC training or gave one or more of the following reasons:

- loss of an instrumental team member
- lack of time to follow through
- lack of organizational support, resources, and/or interest at their home institutions
- a persistent culture of blame at their home institutions
- overly restrictive regulations that do not allow much "wiggle room" or any incentives to do more.

CONTINUATION OF CONTACTS AFTER THE END OF TRAINING

- *Key points:* The graduate trainees varied widely in the extent to which they remained in contact with others from the PSIC; the highest rates of contacts were with their own team members.

PSIC trainees tended to remain in contact with their own team members and to contact the VA in the year following training. To a lesser extent, they remained in contact with other teams in the year following the training. Contact with AHRQ was the least frequent. Proportionately more hospital than state representatives tended to initiate contact with others after the end of their training. Table 2.6 presents trainee-interview responses regarding their contacts with PSIC colleagues, AHRQ, and the VA.

Overall, state team members remained in contact with those from their own teams after the training ended. More than two-thirds of those we interviewed had communicated with their own PSIC team members during the year following the PSIC training. Interactions ranged from occasional emails and telephone calls regarding a specific question to monthly (or even weekly) meetings to check in on the continuation of the team's project. Some team members have seen each other almost daily because they work in the same facility.

Table 2.6
Contact with PSIC Colleagues, AHRQ, and VA after PSIC Training Ended, One-Year Follow-Up Telephone Interviews with Year 1 Trainees, 2005

Contact with:	Percentage of Trainees		
	Total (*N*=38)	State (*N*=15)	Hospital (*N*=23)
Own PSIC team members			
Yes	79%	73%	83%
No	18	20	17
NA	3	7	0
Other PSIC teams			
Yes	39	33	43
No	58	60	57
NA	3	7	0
VA			
Yes	63	47	74
No	34	47	26
NA	3	7	0
AHRQ			
Yes	32	33	30
No	66	60	70
NA	3	7	0

NOTES: Year 1 trainees participated in the 2003–2004 training round.

- Percentages within a category may not sum to 100 percent due to rounding error.
- NA = Not applicable, missing, or don't know. Either not applicable per the respondent, who did not feel the topic was relevant, given his/her specific type of organization or role within that organization; answer missing; or the respondent did not feel he/she could answer the question.

PSIC trainees also drew upon the VA's resources. Nearly two-thirds of those interviewed had contacted the VA in the year following the training's end. A much larger proportion of hospital staff had contacted the VA than had state representatives. Contacts were often in the form of an email or telephone call with a specific question. A few also noted that they used the VA's Web site frequently. With very few exceptions, trainees felt that the VA staff was accessible, responsive, and helpful.

Contact with other PSIC team members and with AHRQ occurred to a lesser extent. Approximately 40 percent of those interviewed had been in contact with other PSIC teams from their training year. A larger proportion of hospitals than state representatives had interacted with other PSIC teams. Such contacts tended to be sporadic—for example, calling or emailing with a specific question if someone was trying to launch a program similar to one existing elsewhere, or impromptu conversations upon running into a colleague at a conference.

Likewise, about one-third of the trainees interviewed (both states and hospitals) had contacted AHRQ. Examples of typical contacts include talking with AHRQ staff at both AHRQ- and non-AHRQ-sponsored (e.g., CMS) conferences, and use of AHRQ's Web site. Several trainees noted that they tended to approach the VA directly with specific questions, given the VA's major role in the actual training. Some remarked that they were not sure whom to approach at AHRQ for help and could use more direction regarding what AHRQ could do to assist with post training and whom to contact. Most who had contacted AHRQ said that staff there had provided helpful and timely responses to their questions.

HELPFULNESS OF PSIC TRAINING AND ADVICE TO OTHERS

- *Key points:* Nearly unanimously, Year 1 participants praised the PSIC training one year after it ended, highlighting the helpfulness of the training and the value of the skills they had learned.

The PSIC graduates reported that the training had been helpful and continued to be helpful in improving processes used to monitor and improve patient safety. The majority of trainees also said they would recommend enthusiastically the PSIC training to other states and hospitals. Participants advised those contemplating participation to assemble a diverse team of senior management, front-line staff, and those involved directly in patient safety efforts from both hospitals and states. They also advised AHRQ and the VA to include representatives from CMS and JCAHO, given their prominent and powerful roles in patient safety, to help them gain greater perspective on the importance of a just culture and how their policies affect providers' ability to pursue patient safety improvements.

Helpfulness of the Training

Overall, with one year's perspective, the Year 1 trainees felt that the PSIC training had been helpful in improving the process(es) they use to monitor and improve patient safety. Trainees were asked to rate the helpfulness of the PSIC training on a scale of 1 to 10, with 1 being not at all helpful and 10 being very helpful. As reported in Table 2.7, 92 percent of participants gave ratings of 7 or higher. Ratings were similarly high for the states (100 percent) and hospitals (87 percent). Those who gave ratings of 6 or less felt that many of the tools were not relevant to their jobs, or had not attended all the sessions. Those who gave higher ratings said that the following aspects of the training most influenced their responses:

- guidance on patient safety culture
- technical training (e.g., RCA, HFMEA, reporting/aggregating data, human factors engineering)
- engaging presenters and dynamic VA staff
- hands-on exercises
- extensive library
- opportunities for networking.

Table 2.7

Helpfulness of PSIC Training and Advice to Others, Reported by the Year 1 Trainees in the One-Year Follow-Up Telephone Interviews

Question About PSIC	Percentage of Trainees		
	Total (*N*=38)	State (*N*=15)	Hospital (*N*=23)
Was the PSIC training helpful in improving processes used to monitor and improve patient safety?			
1-2 (Not at all helpful)	0%	0%	0%
3-4	3	0	4
5-6	3	0	4
7-8	39	40	39
9-10 (Very helpful)	53	60	48
NA	3	0	4
What would you say *to a state* contemplating participation in a PSIC training program?			
1-2 (Not recommend at all)	0	0	0%
3-4	0	0	0
5-6	3	0	4
7-8	5	7	4
9-10 (Recommend enthusiastically)	89	87	91
NA	3	7	0
What would you say *to a hospital or other provider organization* contemplating participation in a PSIC training program?			
1-2 (Not recommend at all)	3	0	4
3-4	0	0	0
5-6	0	0	0
7-8	3	7	0
9-10 (Recommend enthusiastically)	92	93	91
NA	3	0	4

NOTES: Year 1 trainees participated in the 2003–2004 training round.

- Percentages within a category may not sum to 100 percent due to rounding error.
- NA = Not applicable, missing, or don't know. Either not applicable per the respondent, who did not feel the topic was relevant given his/her specific type of organization or role within that organization; answer missing; or the respondent did not feel he/she could answer the question.

We asked PSIC participants what they were doing better, if anything, on a day-to-day basis as a direct result of the PSIC training. Those who said they were doing something better pointed to improvements in the following areas:

- patient safety culture
- evaluating and prioritizing concerns
- self-confidence
- credibility
- being more proactive instead of reactive

- analyzing adverse events and near misses more rigorously and consistently
- educating others
- in general, "looking at everything with a more critical eye," especially with regard to human factors.

These individuals said that improvements had been made possible by the practical skills, technical training, readings, networking, and excellent teachers provided in the PSIC. Those who felt that they were not doing better a year later with regard to patient safety said that they need more ongoing support to make system changes, and that their jobs needed to have more of a clear patient safety focus.

In addition, we asked participants about what they would say to others contemplating participation in the PSIC training program. Also reported in Table 2.7, with one year of hindsight, nearly all the Year 1 trainees (89 percent) said that they would recommend enthusiastically that states attend, and a similar proportion (92 percent) said the same about the attendance of hospitals or other provider organizations. In nearly all cases, respondents noted that there was very little downside to attending and that "these changes are coming whether you like it or not, so you better get on board now, rather than be left behind." In nearly all cases (97 percent [data not shown]), the 2003–2004 participants said that, knowing what they know now, they would participate in the PSIC training. Some even noted that they would like to attend the entire year-long course again as a refresher. Those who responded less enthusiastically questioned the usefulness of the PSIC training for state agencies, given that the tools were geared more to hospitals. These individuals suggested that the VA rework the course to be more relevant to states. A few felt the course was not sophisticated enough to be of value to participants reasonably well versed in the basics of patient safety and suggested that a more advanced course be created.

Finally, in terms of the type of staff that the Year 1 PSIC participants would recommend an organization send to the training in order to maximize impact at home, almost all noted the importance of having a diverse group so that individuals from different backgrounds can begin to understand each other's perspectives and "get on the same page." Almost all of those interviewed strongly urged AHRQ and the VA to allow for larger teams, thereby ensuring wide breadth of expertise, diverse perspectives (e.g., front-line staff and high-ranking managers from states *and* hospitals), and increased potential for "spreading the word." The following specific suggestions were made about the types of personnel to include:

- high-ranking individuals from hospitals (e.g., vice president of medical affairs, CEO, COO [corporate operations officer], CFO [corporate finance officer] and states (e.g., legislators) who have influence and can push for change from the top
- clinicians, including physician and nursing leaders and clinical pharmacists
- patient safety officers and risk managers
- representatives from
    - quality improvement teams
    - state and local hospital associations
    - the state's department of health licensure office, especially those involved in reporting efforts
    - long-term care facilities

- ambulatory care settings
- medical and nursing schools involved in curriculum development
- QIOs
- JCAHO
- CMS.

Trainees repeatedly emphasized the importance of having those in positions of power attend the sessions (e.g., CEOs, elected officials) so that these individuals are motivated to become part of the solution to patient safety problems. We note that AHRQ specifically did not target the CEOs for training because many patient safety training options already are available to them through other programs for health care executives. The suggestions for CEO participation indicate that the PSIC participants were not aware of such alternative training options for CEOs.

Trainees also suggested that representatives from CMS and JCAHO attend the PSIC training. It was thought that participation by CMS and JCAHO staff would help increase their awareness of the importance of having a just culture, rather than a blame environment, and also would help them gain greater perspective on how their policies affect providers' ability to pursue patient safety improvements.

FUTURE TRAINING ACTIVITIES

- *Key points:* Many of the Year 1 PSIC graduates expressed interest in future activities to retain and expand their patient safety knowledge and skills, referring specifically to an interest in participating in training others and in refresher courses for themselves.

Interest of PSIC Graduates in Training Others

In the year since their training ended, many of the Year 1 PSIC graduates—especially hospital representatives—had trained others in patient safety skills and tools. A significant majority also said that they were willing to serve as a trainer to others. To do this in a more formal capacity, trainees noted that they would need assistance from AHRQ and the VA in the form of financial, course-content, and logistical support. The AHRQ/VA partnership anticipated some of these needs and plans to address them through its train-the-trainer course to be held after the completion of the Year 3 PSIC training. The interest expressed by these PSIC graduates in training others suggests that there is a demand for this course. Those who had not trained any staff or were not interested in doing so in the future usually did not feel competent to do so, or felt that assuming the role of trainer was not in the scope of their current positions.

We asked participants whether they had been able to train others within their organization, community, or state in the skills and tools learned through the training. A significant proportion of those we interviewed (87 percent) said yes. Although both responses were high, a larger proportion of hospital representatives (91 percent) than state representatives (80 percent) had trained others.

Those who trained others usually focused on RCA, HFMEA, human factors, and patient safety culture. They often gave presentations to and shared PSIC books and tools with the following:

- internal departments and staff (e.g., house staff, clinical students, risk managers, quality improvement officers, and patient safety committee members)

- other hospitals
- local, regional, or state organizations (e.g., patient safety collaboratives, state hospital association, state boards of medicine and nursing).

Those who did not train others said that they felt unqualified to do so (e.g., limited experience with skills and tools) or that they did not have the time. Some noted that they would have trained others but had changed positions since the training ended to a job for which the subject matter was not relevant.

PSIC participants also seemed quite willing to serve as trainers to others in their state in the future (82 percent). At both the state and hospital representative level, interest was comparably strong, with 87 percent and 78 percent, respectively, indicating that they would train others. However, those willing noted that they would need the following in order to be a trainer, some of which the AHRQ/VA partnership had already planned to include in the upcoming train-the-trainer course:

- outside funding for their time, travel, and teaching supplies
- educational materials from the VA and AHRQ (e.g., slides on different topics that could be tailored as needed)
- reduced work responsibilities in their current jobs, along with support staff to handle administrative details of the training
- a refresher course for the trainers to ensure the currency of their knowledge of patient safety content and tools, and to increase their depth of knowledge on specific techniques.

Although many felt that their organizations would be encouraging of their involvement as trainers, they emphasized the need to obtain clear support from the senior management at their institutions. They also underscored the importance of having this effort be a true partnership among the VA, AHRQ, and the trainers, so that the training would be well coordinated and consistent across the country. One individual suggested that one potential model for funding and supporting this effort may be to form partnerships between the government (i.e., AHRQ and the VA) and the entities wanting to be trained, with each side shouldering some of the costs and logistical coordination of the training effort.

Those not at all interested in or ambivalent about being a trainer thought that they are not qualified to train others or that participation in such training is not relevant to their current positions.

Need for Further Training or Refresher Course

One year after the end of their PSIC training, both hospital and state Year 1 participants were interested in additional patient safety training or some sort of refresher course. Overall, 92 percent said such training would be useful to them. Interest was strong among both state and hospital-affiliated trainees, with 87 percent and 96 percent, respectively, indicating their enthusiasm. Suggestions for content ranged from consultation on individual projects to big-picture updates on new patient safety literature and tools. A preference was expressed for interactive sessions and a program length of one or two days.

Those who were interested in a refresher course made the following suggestions about possible content:

- training about how to use data to guide their local patient safety programs
- practice doing RCAs and HFMEAs and making them effective
- exposure to the PSIs and how best to use them
- consultation on individual projects
- information about return on investment
- direction about how to launch patient safety initiatives in long-term care facilities
- updates on
  - new tools, research, and patient safety activities of both AHRQ and the VA
  - new patient safety technologies.

Suggestions also were made regarding the format of a refresher course. Many said the refresher course would be most helpful if it were structured as a very interactive session with minimal lectures and a significant amount of time devoted to practical exercises and networking. One trainee advised to have concurrent panels on specific topics (e.g., adverse drug reactions, how to engage front-line staff) and let attendees pick which topics are most relevant to them. Almost all those who offered suggestions said that the course should be taken in person rather than virtually, because, in their opinion, conference calls or videoconferencing do not work well for these types of events, and it should not be longer than one or two days. Some noted that, for convenience's sake with regard to travel time and costs, AHRQ may want to contemplate organizing such a refresher course as an add-on to its annual patient safety meeting (either as a pre- or post-meeting session).

Finally, some caveats were noted. Although most who expressed interest in a refresher course said that they could get time off of work to attend, nearly all remarked that they would need funding for travel expenses. They also advised AHRQ and the VA to provide advance notice of the course dates to allow sufficient time to prepare to be out of the office and to "market" the course to senior management to secure their approval.

Chapter 3
Second-Year 2004–2005 Trainees

OVERVIEW OF FINDINGS

As with the Year 1 trainees, the experiences of the Year 2 (2004–2005) PSIC trainees were positive overall. Participants especially appreciated the skills and tools taught during the program; the opportunities to practice those skills; the networking with the PSIC instructors, the VA, and colleagues from other states; the extensive library of books and other materials; and the funding provided by AHRQ.

Similar to findings for the Year 1 training, according to participants' reports, the Year 2 PSIC appears to have facilitated actions by participants to improve patient safety in their home organizations. Considering this finding along with the feedback and actions reported by the Year 1 participants, we can conclude that this program is contributing a growing number of personnel trained in patient safety to a national infrastructure, to help support effective patient safety practices. The Year 2 PSIC graduates have mastered a set of skills and have been sharing the skills and tools learned in the training with others in their immediate organizations, as well as more broadly in their local communities and across their states. They have drawn (and continue to draw) upon these resources to launch new patient safety initiatives and improve existing ones.

Notably, the second-year trainees were more keenly aware than the first-year trainees of the necessity to collaborate with parties once viewed as adversaries (e.g., hospital employees and state regulators). Part of this change is likely attributable to the increased interest in and awareness of patient safety issues nationally and to the ensuing realization by these parties that it behooves them to work together, even if doing so is challenging. According to the Year 2 trainees themselves, the PSIC has played an instrumental role in changing attitudes in this regard, as was anticipated by the AHRQ/VA partnership. The Year 1 group's experiences, coupled with the national trend of increasing awareness of patient safety issues, seem to have paved the way for constructive interactions among the state and hospital representatives in the Year 2 group.

Although the message about the Year 2 PSIC program is generally positive, trainees did continue to experience some barriers, and they offered suggestions for improvements. As with the first-year trainees, the second-year trainees faced limitations of time, funding, and staff in trying to move their patient safety agendas forward. Significant work also remains to be done to change the culture of blame that still exists at many institutions and to secure the buy-in and financial support from senior management to make progress. With regard to improvements in the PSIC course, Year 2 trainees noted the need to train larger, more-diverse teams to increase the odds of spreading the skills and tools and overall patient safety message back home; the need for more direction about effective interventions; and the need to involve national players, such as CMS and JCAHO, in the training. They also underscored the necessity for continued training after the official conclusion of the program—including short sessions geared to busy senior leadership (e.g., CEOs). We note that the AHRQ/VA partnership recognized the importance of involving senior leaders, such as CEOs, but did not gear the PSIC to this audience given that programs designed for these types of individuals already exist.

We present below the detailed findings on the Year 2 trainees from which the above summary assessment was drawn.

FINDINGS FROM THE MAY 2005 TEAM INTERVIEWS

More than 80 trainees from 21 states completed the second year of PSIC training, from September 2004 through May 2005. Nineteen of the states were new to the PSIC training. As a result of their enthusiasm, two states (Maryland and Massachusetts) that participated in the Year 1 training sent new teams to the Year 2 training, and the program had the capacity to include them.

During the third and final session of the training in May 2005, four RAND researchers conducted group interviews with representatives from 12 of the 21 state teams (a total of 45 individuals—20 representing hospitals and 25 representing states). We did not interview all of the teams because of time constraints during the session, and some teams did not want to participate. The teams we interviewed had similar perceptions and feedback about their experiences with the training, giving us confidence in the validity of the information obtained from the interviews. However, some opinions held by the teams not interviewed may not have been captured.

The interviews were designed to assess the participants' experiences with the training, how they were using the training within their organizations, and thoughts for improving the program. A RAND researcher led the discussion with members of each state team that volunteered, using a structured protocol containing a mix of open- and close-ended questions (see Appendix C). Although a substantial number of teams were interviewed, some opinions may not have been captured. The findings from these team interviews are presented below.

Year 2 Team Composition and Formation

- *Key points:* Participants learned about the PSIC in a variety of ways. Many were actively tracking the release of the application, given that they had heard positive feedback about the program from past trainees. The membership of about half the teams was consistent throughout the training; the other half either lost members or, more commonly, had members who missed parts or all of the week-long sessions due to unforeseen circumstances (e.g., illness, changes in employment).

As required in the PSIC training application, teams comprised both state and hospital representatives. More so than with the first-year trainees, the second-year trainees from hospitals tended to hold positions with responsibilities directly related to patient safety (i.e., patient safety coordinator, patient ombudsman), reflecting a national trend of increasing awareness of and importance placed on patient safety. Team members from the state tended to be employed by state health departments in a regulatory capacity (e.g., licensing, inspections, compliance investigation). A number of Year 2 team members were affiliated with QIOs, an increase from one QIO participating in the first year.

Trainees learned about the PSIC program in a variety of ways (e.g., from an email distribution list, by word of mouth from a Year 1 PSIC participant, from a QIO, at a conference). Many teams had heard about the PSIC and were actively tracking the release of the request for application. In most cases, one organization—a state or hospital representative—spearheaded the formation of the team. In all cases, as was required, a state representative took charge of completing the application process.

Consistency of team membership across the training year varied. Five of the 12 teams reported that their original team configuration did not change during the course of the PSIC training. The remaining seven teams did report changes or they had members who missed some parts of the training for a variety of reasons, including illness, weather interference with travel, prior family commitments, conflicts with other work priorities, and changes in employment.

Second-Year 2004–2005 Expectations of the PSIC Training

- *Key points:* Expectations of the Year 2 PSIC trainees at the start of the program varied widely—from some knowing a significant amount about the program, to others who were not sure of the details. All hoped to learn valuable skills. The majority of the Year 2 participants were well aware that the program would be demanding in terms of reading assignments and, especially, the team project. They also recognized that both AHRQ and the VA expected them to share at home what they had learned in the PSIC program.

The initial expectations of the Year 2 PSIC trainees varied widely. Some trainees knew very little about the program, had no expectations, and just "hoped to learn the basics." Others knew some details but not the "full scope of the activities." Still others had high expectations, usually based on their esteem for AHRQ and the VA, on their trust in the entity spearheading their team's PSIC application, or on the positive feedback they had heard from the Year 1 trainees. Regardless of their initial thoughts about the program, most hoped they would be provided with useful tools, skills, and guidance about how to use them.

At the outset, the majority of trainees were well aware of the expectations of AHRQ and the VA. Most knew that the program was intense, involved reading assignments, required the completion of a team project by the third session, and that it included, as part of their responsibility as trainees, helping "spread the word" back home about what they learned. Several noted that they also assumed that AHRQ and the VA wanted them to forge a working relationship between hospitals and state regulators in their states.

Prior Patient Safety Experience of the Second-Year PSIC Participants

- *Key points:* Most trainees had a general understanding of patient safety issues when they started the training, but they were not as familiar with the tools and interventions for ensuring patient safety. About half of the teams came from states with mandatory reporting systems, and they had mixed opinions about the utility of such systems as they currently operated. Those without a reporting system were interested in establishing one, but they foresaw barriers such as lack of funding.

When we asked Year 2 PSIC trainees about their pre-training level of experience across four broad patient safety areas, we found that most had a general understanding of patient safety issues, but more limited experience with tools and interventions. Table 3.1 presents our interview findings regarding trainees' patient safety experience before the start of the Year 2 PSIC program. Regarding general knowledge of medical errors and patient safety, most trainees (71 percent) said they entered the PSIC program with an expertise level of 3 or 4 out of 5 (on a 1-to-5 scale, with 1 being no experience at all and 5 being a high level of experience); one-fifth (20 percent) said they had a high level of expertise in this area.

By comparison, trainees rated themselves as less experienced with tools used to investigate patient safety issues (e.g., near misses, medical errors, patient harm): Most (67 percent) gave themselves a 2 or 3 out of 5; only 2 percent said they were highly experienced in this area. For experience with interventions to improve patient safety, and with evaluation techniques, approximately one-quarter rated themselves as a 2; another one-third rated themselves as a 3; and close to one-third (29 percent and 27 percent, respectively) rated themselves as a 4. Approximately 10 percent or less of the trainees said that they either had no experience or a high level of experience in these two areas. There were no discernable differences detected between the responses of hospital and state representatives.

Table 3.1
Prior Experience with Patient Safety for the Year 2 PSIC Trainees

Content Area	Percentage of Trainees by Level of Prior Experience (*N*=45)				
	1 (None)	2	3	4	5 (High)
Medical error, patient safety, and the risks and hazards in the system leading to patient injury due to the delivery of health care	4%	4%	38%	33%	20%
Tools used to investigate near misses, medical errors, and patient harm/injury resulting from the delivery of health care	13	29	38	18	2
Interventions to improve patient safety or reduce/mitigate the impact of medical errors	7	24	33	29	7
Evaluation techniques to assess the impact of programs, or interventions to improve patient safety and reduce the opportunity for medical errors and their impact	4	24	33	27	11

NOTES: Percentages within a category may not sum to 100 percent due to rounding error.
Year 2 trainees participated in the 2004–2005 training round.

Regarding past experience, we also asked the Year 2 trainees about their state reporting systems (or lack thereof). Of the 12 teams interviewed, half came from states that have statewide reporting systems, most of which are mandatory. Feelings were mixed about the utility of the information obtained from such systems. While some trainees said that their reporting system was helpful for a variety of purposes—such as general tracking, verification of information, and generation of advisories to problematic institutions or individuals—others did not find their reporting system useful, owing to the continued vagueness around definitions of certain data elements and the current lack of longitudinal data. Some trainees mentioned that a significant hurdle to using the data is the lack of analytic resources (e.g., time, trained staff); additionally, at least one state team noted that it was too early to judge the utility of its system, given that it was only recently implemented.

We also asked state teams with reporting systems if the PSIC training had made them want to alter anything about their current reporting system. Many of these trainees replied yes and noted the following areas they would like to address:

- adding nursing homes to the mandatory reporting effort
- standardizing information submitted as part of required RCAs, including defining a structured investigation procedure for all hospitals to use

- using RCA data more
- standardizing patient safety definitions
- analyzing trend data
- offering feedback to entities that provide direct patient care (such as hospitals, ambulatory clinics) about measures to support patient safety–related quality improvement efforts
- strengthening corrective action so that it is instructive, rather than solely punitive
- working more with schools of medicine and/or nursing and professional societies to educate students about the importance of reporting, and how to do it in constructive ways.

As far as actual changes made to reporting systems as a result of the PSIC, most trainees with reporting systems noted that they had not yet had time to implement changes, but that the PSIC training had helped put "key issues on our radar screens" regarding reporting systems and that their participation in the program gave them "focus, legitimacy, credibility, and enhanced skills" that assisted them upon their return home. One state team had conducted training for hospitals about reporting systems that drew upon some of the areas addressed in the PSIC training. At least one trainee expressed a wish that the PSIC had provided more guidance about how to extract useful information out of existing reporting systems, how to push politically for reporting system changes, what good and bad reporting systems look like, and what makes reporting systems good. Several noted that an important barrier to being able to make any changes to existing reporting systems, despite the best intentions, is lack of funding.

Most of the members of teams from states without a reporting system said that they were interested in working to implement one in theory, but in practice they foresaw significant challenges, including lack of funding, political opposition, and liability issues. Also, several individuals from QIOs stated that they would be unable to participate in or lead a commission or group to establish a reporting system because they are supposed to be politically neutral. Nevertheless, many of these teams mentioned that they were encouraged by the progress of other states in overcoming such challenges, and some had plans to pursue more in-depth conversations with states that might serve as models for their own.

CONTENT OF THE SECOND-YEAR PSIC TRAINING

Feedback on the Training Contents

- *Key points:* The Year 2 PSIC participants felt that the information provided at the sessions and in the readings and homework was geared to the appropriate level. The networking was also valued highly and viewed as an important part of the course. The majority of trainees took very seriously the responsibility of sharing information with colleagues back home and was already taking steps on this front during the training year. By the end of the third Year 2 PSIC training session, the overwhelming majority of participants reported having a high skill level across major patient safety areas and felt that their team had been successful in conducting their PSIC project, despite challenges. Trainees tended to draw upon the VA and their peers for help; they appreciated the VA phone meetings, but had several suggestions for making them more useful.

Overall, PSIC participants felt the information provided during the training and in the readings/homework was geared to the appropriate level. In contrast to the preceding year, when many participants felt overwhelmed by the volume, this year's trainees considered the amount of work doable—although they did note that it was often challenging to find the time to complete the assignments, given other work responsibilities. Homework was frequently completed on their own time (i.e., evenings, weekends).

As to criticisms and suggestions with regard to the class content, many trainees voiced appreciation for the extensive library, but suggested that future training refer to the specifics of the assignments. They felt that often they would read an assignment without receiving any supplemental commentary or direction about the important take-home points from it. They suggested that the presenters—whom many said were excellent—be advised to make more of an effort to link their talks to the assigned readings on their given topic. Some found the statistical courses to be "far too technical" and suggested gearing these to much more of a layman's audience. A few PSIC participants said that they would have liked to learn about HFMEA earlier in the training year "to help tie all the pieces together" sooner. Some also noted that although they had heard about and/or used some of the skills and tools taught in the training, they found it useful to hear about topics again (i.e., "repetition is a good thing"), especially from the VA's perspective.

Several trainees noted that the breakout groups did not work well if members of the group were not engaged. In particular, it was suggested that the RCA workshops be run by a facilitator. Also, some trainees did not find it useful to randomly place individuals in groups to carry out practice exercises, given that some groups ended up entirely with people who were not knowledgeable or engaged. Trainees also advised against "re-mixing up" groups because doing so led to more confusion and lack of continuity.

Finally, with regard to course content, several participants felt that representatives from CMS should have been present. Trainees feel that CMS's input is valuable, so being able to hear from that agency would have been a useful part of the course content throughout the three weeks of training. They also underscored the importance of including representatives from JCAHO, long-term care facilities, ambulatory care settings, and medical/nursing schools involved in curriculum development, for similar reasons.

The Optional Telephone Meetings

The IAA included an expert technical assistance component and the telephone meetings, with optional participation, were facilitated by the VA. The calls were designed to provide technical assistance and support to PSIC participants and to provide a vehicle for exchange of ideas and experiences among participating teams.

Many of the teams had not used these calls, but some teams had participated in them regularly.

We heard mixed opinions on the utility of the optional telephone meetings from the Year 2 PSIC participants who had joined in the calls. Trainees appreciated that the calls were offered on multiple days and times, making it easier for those in different time zones and with complex schedules to be involved. They appreciated the chance to come together as a larger team, especially at the beginning, when there was confusion about picking a project topic, to hear about each other's projects and to learn about each other's struggles. Of particular note, trainees valued the frequent access to the VA staff and the respectful manner in which the calls were managed (i.e., "no such thing as a stupid question").

On the negative side, some trainees felt that the calls were often too short to get into any useful details, or that discussions were often not relevant to them because the team projects were so diverse. The calls also tended to be dominated by certain individuals, which made it so that others were not able to speak. In addition, they felt that there were too many project updates and not enough interaction, especially later in the training year. Trainees offered several suggestions to improve the telephone interactions:

- It would be very useful to have a clear agenda sent out before each call, especially at the beginning, when individuals do not know each other and are not yet fully engaged in their projects. Trainees suggested that the VA ask for topic suggestions via email before each series of calls and that, periodically, a summary of key points to be discussed on the calls be sent out to the entire group for the benefit of those not able to attend.

- The first 10 or 15 minutes of each telephone meeting should be an open discussion among trainees without the VA or AHRQ present. The purpose of this segment of the call would be to let teams have a chance to chat about concerns that some may not feel comfortable raising with the PSIC organizers without first getting a read from peers.

- The VA should suggest to teams that they rotate attendees so that someone from each team is usually on each call and no one team member is charged with attending every call (which can be burdensome time-wise).

- Alternatives or complements to the telephone meetings were suggested, including an online chat room or email distribution list and videoconferencing to allow for more personal interactions.

- One VA staff person should be assigned to each team and tasked with setting up periodic check-in calls with their assigned teams. Some felt that this individual consultation with each team would be more useful and efficient than the group telephone conversations.

Those who did not participate in the calls or joined very infrequently said lack of time was a significant factor. These individuals often noted that receiving an agenda enough in advance of the call would be helpful and would likely allow them to participate more often. An agenda would enable them to determine whether they would find the call relevant and, if so, to plan their schedules accordingly.

In addition to the telephone meetings, the Year 2 PSIC participants found other interactions useful. The overwhelming majority of those who said they contacted VA staff found them very helpful and responsive. The much lesser number who contacted AHRQ staff also were extremely complimentary about the help they received. Interactions among trainees' own team members were frequently cited as being useful. Trainees also found it useful to talk to other states conducting similar projects and frequently used the contact list provided by the VA to do so. Some suggested that AHRQ provide a comprehensive list of all AHRQ-funded patient safety projects (i.e., not just PSIC) and contact information for project leads for each project. Many found it difficult to learn about other AHRQ-funded grantees and thought that learning about some of AHRQ's non-PSIC patient safety work could have helped them with their PSIC projects, as well as with other ongoing patient safety efforts in their organizations and states. Another suggestion was to have periodic PSIC reunions to help trainees maintain and expand their networks, and to keep abreast of patient safety literature and innovative projects.

SKILLS AND PROJECTS DEVELOPED BY THE TRAINEES

Applying the Skills at Home

When asked if they had used any of the skills or tools taught during the PSIC in their current jobs, many Year 2 trainees said that they were conducting improved RCAs and HFMEAs as a result of their PSIC courses, sometimes despite significant resistance from staff and management regarding the time involved to adhere to the VA's rigorous methods. They reported using the laminated instruction cards often and visiting the Web sites of both AHRQ and the VA. They also said that the human factors knowledge and the new way of looking at patient safety issues coming out of the PSIC program "infiltrate everything [we] do." As expected, those trainees not working in clinical settings did not use tools geared toward clinical applications, but they did report using the nonclinical tools (e.g., building a business case).

The majority of trainees seemed to take the responsibility of sharing information with colleagues back home very seriously. Most said that they were actively sharing the books and other course materials with their staff; trainees not working in clinical settings said that they made an effort to tell their clinical colleagues about tools that may be relevant to them. Several trainees said they had plans to use PSIC skills and tools as part of presentations to the following: staff at monthly meetings (e.g., performance improvement and risk management committee meetings), senior management, broader audiences (e.g., state risk management societies and local conferences), and staff at nursing home/long-term care facilities, where many trainees said the culture is still very punitive. Appreciation was voiced for the fact that the PSIC helped prompt collaboration between states and hospitals, making conversations and sharing between such organizations easier and more meaningful. Regarding the sharing of information, the main area in which trainees seemed to be having difficulty was time; as one trainee remarked, "It is so hard for so few people to go back and make big changes—we need more people [from each organization] to attend the training!"

By the end of the Year 2 PSIC training, the overwhelming majority of participants reported having a high skill level across the five areas we asked about: selecting appropriate tools, conducting an investigation of medical errors/near misses and preparing a report, developing an intervention, measuring and evaluating the impact of the intervention, and translating interventions into standard clinical practice. Across all of these categories, between 76 and 92 percent of respondents rated their skill level as either a 4 or a 5 on a 5-point scale, with 1 being not at all skilled and 5, very skilled. Table 3.2 presents the self-reported skill level of trainees at the end of the 2004–2005 PSIC training in a variety of key areas. (Comparable data were not collected on the Year 1 trainees. Given that the evaluation goals of the first year were exploratory, we tracked only the initial experiences and dynamics of the PSIC program.)

Table 3.2
Skill Levels Reported by Year 2 Trainees at the End of the Year 2 PSIC Training

Content Area	Percentage of Trainees Reporting Skill Level at the End of PSIC Training (*N*=45)				
	1 (None)	2	3	4	5 (Very skilled)
Select the appropriate tool(s) to investigate an error or near miss.	0%	0%	9%	56%	36%
Conduct an investigation of a medical error or near miss and prepare reports based on your findings.	0	0	11	56	33
Develop an intervention based on the findings from your investigation.	0	0	16	62	22
Measure and evaluate the impact of the safety intervention you developed.	2	0	16	58	24
Translate patient safety interventions into standard clinical practice.	0	2	22	60	16

NOTES: Percentages within a category may not sum to 100 percent due to rounding error.

Year 2 trainees participated in the 2004–2005 training round.

The Projects Conducted by the 2004–2005 Trainees

As with the Year 1 trainees, the projects of the Year 2 PSIC participants were diverse. However, in comparison with those of the first year, the Year 2 project topics were more applied and appeared to address issues that the institutions were well aware needed attention, as was encouraged by the AHRQ/VA partnership. As a result, these projects were less focused on methods and more focused on tackling real-world problems. They had less the character of churning out a homework assignment to prove the attainment of a skill set and more that of applying skills and tools in realistic ways to genuine concerns. For example, the Massachusetts team developed a specific program based upon clinical evidence to prevent central venous catheter (i.e., "central-line") infections, and implemented this program in several intensive care units (ICUs). Additionally, to a greater extent than the prior year, many Year 2 teams focused on changing patient safety culture.

Overall, although faced with limited time in which to complete their projects, the Year 2 teams appeared to be less rushed and to face fewer internal conflicts than did the Year 1 group, perhaps because many of them already had well-formed ideas for projects as they started the training, and plans for how to execute them, from talking to last year's PSIC graduates. In addition, by the time the second training started, the national health care community was more aware of the need for patient safety improvements than it had been a year ago, which would help focus and reinforce the work of the second trainee group. Table 3.3 presents the titles of each Year 2 PSIC team's project.

All of the teams we interviewed felt their team had been successful in conducting its PSIC project. However, the Year 2 trainees frequently mentioned that they still had work to do and had plans to do it. There was a strong sense that the work they did for the PSIC project was "just the beginning," and that the project would continue after the training ended.

As with the Year 1 trainees, the Year 2 trainees mentioned many challenges in carrying out their team projects. In particular, the challenge of juggling time to work on the PSIC project with ongoing job commitments was mentioned quite often, although most said their superiors were supportive of their PSIC project-related responsibilities. Table 3.4 outlines the most frequently mentioned challenges, gives examples of each, and notes how the team(s) tried to overcome them, if possible. Of note, several trainees remarked that lack of CEO support would have been a significant impediment, but this was not an issue because of AHRQ's requirement that each participating institution provide a clear statement of support for and understanding of the level of commitment. Many felt this requirement was key to the support they received at home and that the support statement provided a useful document to refer to if problems arose. This response, when compared with the first-year participants' identification of lack of CEO commitment as a barrier, suggests that awareness of patient safety issues by hospital leadership may have heightened during that period, thus leading to stronger CEO support for the second group of trainees.

USE OF THE PSIC TRAINING BY THE SECOND-YEAR TRAINEES

Highlights of Findings

The most frequently mentioned skills and tools taught through the PSIC that were used by the trainees to carry out their team projects were RCA, HFMEA, and patient safety culture survey/just culture materials. Trainees also reported that they had implemented initiatives as a result of the PSIC (e.g., conducting training courses locally), were using PSIC skills and tools in their daily practice, and anticipated more use in the future. Lack of time, too few staff, and inadequate funding were the key barriers trainees mentioned to using the PSIC skills and tools on a regular basis. The self-assessed comfort level of trainees with the different types of data and methods taught during the PSIC training was mixed; usually those in clinical settings with more opportunities to practice the methods felt more confident.

Table 3.3
Team Projects of the Year 2 PSIC Trainees

State	Project Title
California	Patient Safety Improvement Resource Manual
District of Columbia	A Focused Assessment of the Culture of Safety in Two Hospitals in the District of Columbia
Florida	Dissemination of the Data Analysis of Wrong Site, Wrong Patient, Wrong Procedure Code 15 Reports to Florida Hospitals and Ambulatory Surgical Centers in an Effort to Increase Patient Safety
Georgia	Correct Site, Correct Patient Surgeries and Procedures—Successful Practices in Georgia
Hawaii	Pa'a Lima—Working Together with Pride and Mutual Trust
Idaho	Medication Reconciliation Model Critical Access Hospital Inpatient Admissions
Indiana	Deep Vein Thrombosis and Glucose Monitoring
Kentucky	Failure Mode and Effect Analysis (FMEA) as a Measurement Tool to Evaluate the Initiative, Bar Errors by Bar-Coding
Maryland	Nursing Home Root Cause Analysis Project
Massachusetts	Prevention of Central Line Infections—Massachusetts Public-Private Collaboration
Michigan	Hospital Root Cause In-Depth Analysis & Facility Design Standards
Mississippi	Decreasing Health Care Associated Infections Through Initiation of Bundles/Improving the Culture of Safety in the State of Mississippi
Nebraska	The Heart of Safe Care at Fremont Area Medical Center
New Jersey	New Jersey Patient Safety Improvement Corps Team Summary: Development of a System for Patient Safety Reporting and RCAs
North Dakota	Medication Reconciliation
Ohio	Development of an Error Analysis Process Using Existing Databases
South Dakota	Medication Safety: Reconciliation of Medication upon Admission, Transfer and Discharge
Tennessee	Creating a Culture of Safety in the Hospital Setting
Vermont	Developing Statewide Standards for Patient Safety—A Collaborative Approach
Washington	Promoting and Sustaining a Learning Culture Throughout Washington
West Virginia	Factors in Reducing Falls in Health Care Institutions

NOTE: Year 2 trainees participated in the 2004–2005 training round.

Table 3.4

Challenges Experienced by the Year 2 (2004–2005) PSIC Trainees in Conducting Their PSIC Projects

Challenges	Examples of Challenges	Ways Teams Addressed Challenges
Balancing PSIC project work with other job commitments	Competing PSIC project and other work deadlines	Juggled priorities as possible; sought support from superiors as needed; made PSIC team meetings run efficiently (e.g., clear agendas).
Initial determination of project topic and scope	Started one project but had to readjust significantly or completely change topic midway through due to lack of feasibility and/or internal support	No solution mentioned; suggested that PSIC instructors provide clearer or more guidance earlier in the training about project topic selection
Lack of accountability at home institution(s) for engagement in PSIC project	Some departments resistant to change and were not interested in the PSIC project ("inertia is a powerful force!")	Educated and engaged skeptics as much as possible to secure support; would like more representatives from each institution to attend the PSIC training so it is not only one person per institution spearheading the intervention.
Lack of organization within PSIC team	Missed meetings; no clear accountability on tasks	Appointed a PSIC team leader whose jobs it was to call meetings, ensure tasks were clearly assigned and carried out on time, etc.
Geographic distance from PSIC team members	Team members too far away from each other to have regular face-to-face meetings.	Held frequent telephone/videoconference meetings and used email.
Obtaining institutional approval to conduct a survey	Time-consuming human subjects committee review	Importance of such review was recognized; no solutions were suggested
Turnover of members on PSIC team	PSIC team member leaves his/her position or institution and is replaced midway through training by someone else	No solutions were suggested
Time needed to establish relationships on PSIC team	Different interpersonal communication and work styles of team members	No solutions were suggested
Inadequate time to fully implement project	Barely "out of the gate" with the project by the time the PSIC course finished	Sought/are seeking internal support for continuation of the project post PSIC; plan to pursue outside grant funding as well, but lack grant-writing skills

54

Actions Taken as a Result of the Training

The most frequently mentioned skills and tools taught through the PSIC that were used by the trainees to carry out their team projects were RCA, HFMEA, and the patient safety culture survey or other culture materials. Some teams also drew upon the data analysis techniques they were taught and on such assessment tools as the VA's SAC. Several also noted that their projects had a broad scope; thus, they did not focus on one or two skills and tools, but, instead, drew upon the wide range of information to which the training exposed them—including both the skills and tools noted previously and general information, such as patient safety definitions, reporting system guides, and other educational materials.

When asked if they had implemented any initiatives as a result of their participation in the PSIC, many replied affirmatively. Frequently, the Year 2 PSIC participants had been involved in designing and/or carrying out training programs for various types of staff in their institutions (e.g., clinical house staff, medical or nursing students) or beyond (e.g., state organizations). Topics of these educational programs ranged from technical lessons about how to conduct an RCA, to instruction regarding establishing or refining a reporting system, to training exercises in just culture. A few noted that the PSIC had led them to strive for regulatory changes in their state or better implementation of existing laws. Some said that they had started processes to feed data back to hospital associations and regulatory agencies to encourage improvement. Finally, some noted that, as a result of the PSIC training, they had completely redesigned how they conducted RCAs or reported errors at their institutions.

Others said that, although they were not doing anything new as a result of the PSIC, they were doing what they had been doing better and more efficiently (e.g., RCA, HFMEA). Those who had not implemented any initiatives said that they had not yet had the time (because they were intensely engaged in carrying out their team project) or they are not involved in direct patient care, so it is harder for them to find the opportunity to use the skills and tools.

Use of the PSIC Skills and Tools

Most trainees said that they anticipated using the PSIC skills and tools once the training had ended. In particular, they thought they would draw upon the information related to RCA, HFMEA, human factors engineering, and general safety principles. They thought the understanding gained about the VA's approach across many areas would be especially useful. In regard to specific items, trainees said they expected to use frequently the library of books, slides from talks, handouts, and laminated instructional books or cards. They also anticipated referring to information about other states' PSIC projects and drawing upon their new network of colleagues and new spirit of collaboration between states and hospitals.

The overwhelming majority of the Year 2 trainees said that they already had been using the provided PSIC materials in their day-to-day work activities. The most frequently mentioned skills and tools were as follows:

- the library of books (especially *To Err Is Human, The Design of Everyday Things*, and *The Veterans Health Administration [VHA] National Patient Safety Improvement Handbook*)

- course lecture notes (especially regarding RCA, human factors engineering, and the business case for patient safety)

- flip charts and laminated cards

- tools about how to be a facilitator
- assessment tools (e.g., patient safety culture survey)
- the Web sites of AHRQ and the VA NCPS.

We asked the Year 2 trainees if they had undertaken any efforts to systematically assess patient safety culture in hospitals around their state. Some replied yes, noting that the AHRQ tool was particularly useful because it is well done and free, and also that, while they did not always have time to do a complete culture survey, they did try to put culture questions into surveys on other, broader topics. Those who had attempted to assess patient safety culture reported that results varied widely, especially by department (e.g., ICUs tended to score higher, seemingly because they are more attuned to patient safety issues). Many noted that, although scores were sometimes higher than expected, overall "we are not where we'd like to be."

Those who had not assessed culture said that such measurement was either not applicable to their nonclinical jobs or that they did not have the time, funding, staff, and/or support to administer a survey. These individuals also noted that there is still much cynicism about the utility of such surveys (i.e., lip service to being committed to culture when in reality the organization still punishes the individual instead of focusing on system issues).

Barriers or Issues Encountered

The Year 2 PSIC participants encountered a variety of barriers to implementing the skills and tools learned through the training, many of which were similar to those encountered while trainees were carrying out their PSIC team projects. The most frequently mentioned barrier was time. Some noted that the VA's SAC help them prioritize and deal with this challenge. Next was lack of staffing—especially individuals educated in patient safety culture and analytic techniques. Scarce funding also was an issue, especially for small facilities and to support internal training of inexperienced staff. Regarding internal training, trainees noted that in-depth training is difficult to do in large groups. The many smaller courses that are needed require more funding and more staff time. Other challenges that were mentioned include changing patient safety culture and clinicians' behaviors, securing the support of senior management, lack of automated data collection, and underreporting of events.

The trainees reported mixed levels of comfort in working with the different types of data and methods taught during the PSIC training. Some trainees (especially those with prior experience) felt very confident in their abilities to use the skills/tools; others were less confident (especially with regard to data analysis). Lack of adequate statistical support was sometimes mentioned, as was the need for more technical training and support for ongoing projects. Those not working in clinical settings tended to feel less sure of themselves, because they have fewer opportunities to practice their newly learned skills in real-world settings. Still others said that they would feel more at ease using the materials if they had better data to back up their efforts and more knowledge of the literature supporting the types of interventions they wanted to implement in order to counter skeptics.

As a final note about the Year 2 training, although the group was larger than that in the prior training year (21 teams in the second year; 15 in the first year), the training ran smoothly and did not seem to suffer from the increased number of participants. In fact, the larger group appeared to provide more networking opportunities and more exposure to diverse projects and experiences.

SUGGESTIONS FROM TRAINEES FOR FUTURE PROGRAM

Suggestions for Program Content

The Year 2 trainees offered the following suggestions for program content to enhance the PSIC training:

- Reporting systems (e.g., characteristics of "good" and "bad" systems, advice on how to use data more effectively to encourage change)
- Patient safety leadership (i.e., tactics to create and/or improve the patient safety leaders in an institution)
- Patient safety in long-term care and nursing home facilities
- Business case for patient safety (i.e., analytic techniques, ways to best present to senior management)
- Positive corrective actions (e.g., give examples and suggestions)
- Actions state employees can take to improve patient safety. (Some attendees felt that the program was very hospital-centric—important in that some state employees said they left not knowing what they could actively go back and do in their jobs.)
- Human factors analysis of equipment (i.e., more examples)
- Implementation suggestions (some attendees felt that there was too much time spent doing analyses and not enough time on implementing interventions known to work. They would like more direction regarding interventions and how to implement them back home with limited staff).
- Practice doing RCAs
- A guidebook from the VA and AHRQ about the key stakeholders and players in the patient safety field and what they do (their names, resources, stances on certain issues, what they have done, etc.)
- Guidance regarding how to form state patient safety coalitions
- Guidance regarding how to effectively talk to state legislators
- Information on patient safety metrics and when it is best to use each ("You can never get enough of this!")
- Guidance regarding how to launch patient safety education programs in medical and nursing schools and the course content.
- Grant-writing workshop so that projects can continue after the end of the PSIC training and to help trainees obtain funding for new projects
- Academic advisers/methods consultants to individual projects to assist trainees in making projects more rigorous.

Suggestions for Future Program Design

Projecting into the future, the Year 2 trainees said that they thought the following aspects of the PSIC would prove most valuable:

- Training about RCA, HFMEA, just culture, human factors engineering, and requirements for reporting

- Comprehensive PSIC library and resulting knowledge about who the experts are in the patient safety field

- Management philosophies (e.g., getting states and hospitals to collaborate, focusing on the system versus the individual).

A significant portion of those interviewed said that one of the most important—but perhaps less readily tangible or quantifiable—aspects of the training was the exposure to other states' activities and the networks of colleagues each created throughout the country. Other comments centered on the credibility that the trainees felt they had gained from having gone through the PSIC course.

Lastly, even those entering the training from organizations that were already reasonably far down the patient safety path agreed with the above assessments. As one trainee noted, "It's not so much that [our state] would have done different things without the PSIC; it's more that because of the PSIC we will now do them better." Overall, trainees repeatedly voiced that they valued the fact that, no matter where they started, the PSIC training "brought us to another level of awareness of patient safety," and that it was invaluable to talk with others also engaged in the struggle to make patient safety changes (i.e., "we are not alone").

Trainees also suggested that the VA and AHRQ involve more sharp-end clinical staff as well as representatives from CMS and JCAHO to attend the PSIC training. Many trainees felt that there were too many administrators and not enough front-line staff present—that it was critical for clinicians, especially physicians, to take more ownership of their role in improving patient safety and that more patient safety leaders with clinical backgrounds need to be trained. Regarding CMS and JCAHO, a significant number of trainees felt that the training program suffered from a lack of engagement with these two significant players, to help them gain a greater perspective on the importance of a just culture and how their policies affect providers' ability to pursue patient safety improvements.

Chapter 4
Conclusions and Recommendations

Overall, the PSIC program has been very successful. As outlined in this report, statements from the first two groups of trainees have consistently presented a program that is well organized, informative, and worth attending. In particular, trainees report that they are using the skills and tools they learned through the program to make meaningful changes at their home institutions and in their home states, as well as to educate others. They repeatedly have expressed appreciation to AHRQ for financially supporting the PSIC and to the VA for its execution.

Through its funding of the PSIC, AHRQ is helping to build a national infrastructure of skilled personnel that is increasing patient safety awareness and influencing patient safety practices. With increasing awareness of patient safety issues in this country and growing numbers of initiatives by key players (e.g., Leapfrog, Institute for Healthcare Improvement [IHI], JCAHO), resistance to efforts addressing patient safety concerns at the local levels is likely to decline. The PSIC is making important contributions to creating more-receptive and better-informed climates by training a group of well-informed and educated individuals who are currently "spreading the word" in their local communities and throughout their states.

Part of the success of the PSIC to date is a direct result of both AHRQ's and the VA's high level of responsiveness in real time to suggestions for improvement from participants. For example, the PSIC was originally geared to state staff, to help them develop patient safety knowledge and skills. However, at the request of the state participants, hospital representatives were included in the training as well. The resulting interdisciplinary nature of the teams—which were comprised of individuals from a variety of institutions, with a wide range of interests and challenges related to patient safety—proved to be an integral and vital aspect of the PSIC. Additionally, AHRQ and the VA listened to suggestions from Year 1 trainees to make some aspects of the program less technical; as a result, the program in place for Year 2 trainees included modifications that made some courses more applied.

Many PSIC graduates expressed interest in becoming trainers by participating in the planned PSIC train-the-trainer program. They offered specific suggestions regarding what resources they would need to meaningfully assume the role of a trainer. As noted previously in this report, these suggestions include but are not limited to outside funding for time, travel, and teaching supplies; educational materials from the VA and AHRQ (e.g., slides on different topics that could be tailored as needed); reduced work responsibilities in their current jobs; support staff to handle administrative details; and a refresher course for the trainers. They also underscored the importance of having this effort be a true partnership among the VA, AHRQ, and the trainers so that the training would be well coordinated and consistent across the country. This vision is consistent with AHRQ's plan for the train-the-trainer portion of the PSIC program.

Trainees from both years noted that AHRQ did not have a visible presence during the training. Trainees expressed an interest in hearing about a number of AHRQ's patient safety aspects: its broader portfolio of patient safety projects (i.e., beyond PSIC), how the PSIC fits into its broader patient safety goals, what AHRQ has learned across all its projects to date, and its plans for funding patient safety projects in the near term. Trainees asked that AHRQ provide a comprehensive list of all its patient safety projects, with contact information for key researchers and staff to enable PSIC trainees to network with these individuals as well as with their own PSIC peers. We believe that it would be valuable for AHRQ to have a one-hour presentation during the training to update PSIC trainees regarding AHRQ-funded patient safety research and to place the PSIC into the larger context of other AHRQ-funded patient safety research. AHRQ reports that this update has been added to the second session for the third PSIC training cycle.

SUGGESTIONS FOR ACTION BY AHRQ

Based on our assessment of the PSIC at this time, our key suggestions for AHRQ action are the following:

- **Building on the successful PSIC training that has reached the important audience of front-line hospital and state-level staff, AHRQ should now consider alternative education models to engage key decisionmakers who are needed to achieve patient safety improvements (e.g., senior management, state legislators), with a focus on information about the business case for safety and quality, as well as on managing organizational constraints to achieving improvements.**

The intensive training model used for the PSIC has been designed to train front-line hospital and state-level staff (i.e., clinicians providing direct patient care), and it has been very effective in doing so. However, as the trainees reported in our interviews, they cannot make needed changes at the care-delivery level without resources and policies provided to support them. To make meaningful and lasting changes, front-line staff need the support of key decisionmakers—the individuals with authority to make policy and resource decisions (e.g., senior management, state legislators). Training programs already have been made available by other organizations for some audiences (e.g., hospital CEOs). But for other audiences, appropriately designed training options are not yet available. AHRQ should consider which audiences are most important to address, and then gear a modified PSIC program to the busy schedules of these decisionmakers. This can help engage and educate a broader set of health care players about patient safety so that individuals at all levels of the system are "on the same page" and moving toward similar goals. For example, a Web-based or one-day in-person short course could offer executives the knowledge to help them make informed decisions about patient safety policy and practices.

- **AHRQ should provide continued limited support to the PSIC graduates to help them remain engaged in patient safety issues, keep their skills and knowledge current, and encourage cross-fertilization among the PSIC graduates as well as between graduates and others in the field.**

AHRQ should continue to support its original investment in training for the core group of PSIC graduates so that initial gains in patient safety knowledge and skills are retained and further improvements can be made. AHRQ might offer periodic refresher courses in flexible formats (e.g., Web-based training, telephone conference calls, in-person short courses), and it also could provide ongoing access to technical assistance and opportunities for interactions among PSIC graduates. This follow-up support should adapt to the changing needs of the PSIC graduates over time.

SUGGESTIONS FOR FUTURE PROGRAM DESIGN

Given our assessment of the PSIC and the feedback from the first two groups of trainees, we offer the following suggestions for AHRQ and the VA to consider for future PSIC direction and program design.

- **Streamline tools for easier use.** Many trainees noted that, although the techniques taught in the PSIC are impressive for their rigor and are preferred in an ideal world, the time and staff required for conducting the rigorous analyses often made the techniques impractical for use. Therefore, many trainees said they modify these techniques for their purposes, which is consistent with the advice the VA had given them during the training, to adapt the tools to their purposes. Given this fairly broad-based sentiment, it would be advisable for AHRQ and the VA to provide guidance to trainees on how tools can be modified to avoid losing the meaningful components while aiding ease of use.

- **Provide clearer tools and action items to state representatives.** Many state representatives felt that while the PSIC training was very informative and extremely worthwhile from a general-education standpoint, they did not leave the training with many skills and tools that were directly applicable in their positions back home. AHRQ and the VA should rework some aspects of the PSIC training to be more relevant to states, thereby helping provide them with clear action items they can implement independent of hospitals. Some suggested topics include making a business case for patient safety from the state's perspective (e.g., Medicaid savings), cost-effectiveness analyses for state policymaking, and how to establish a statewide patient safety coalition.

- **Seek creative ways to provide training or other information on grant writing to prepare the PSIC graduates to obtain the funding needed to achieve sustainable patient safety practices and programs.** Many PSIC trainees noted that, by the end of their training, they were motivated to continue their PSIC projects and to launch new efforts. However, they also underscored the significant limitation of internal funds and their inexperience in writing grants to obtain outside funding. Ultimately, health care organizations should be making safety improvements as a normal course of business, without seeking external funding to subsidize their efforts. Yet, in some cases, such as when an organization is pursuing unique solutions, additional funding may be justified. AHRQ should consider developing training on grant writing, such as a short course or online training resources, to guide trainees on how and where to seek funding. If funding permits, and if circumstances indicate that additional resources would help support new approaches, AHRQ should also consider funding short-term, small-scale grants geared to furthering projects of recent PSIC graduates. Some trainees said that as little as $10,000 would help them push their projects forward in meaningful ways.

- **Implement the train-the-trainer program as a working partnership among AHRQ, the VA, and the trainers to ensure that new trainers have the needed teaching skills and resources to support their activities.** Continued diffusion of the skills and tools taught through the PSIC is critical to its long-term success and impact. A train-the-trainer program offers the potential to encourage such diffusion by leveraging AHRQ resources into the field through the trainers. The training activities have two potential audiences: (1) staff at each trainer's home institution and (2) staff in other organizations that have not received any PSIC training, e.g., ambulatory clinics, state medical societies, long-term care providers, insurers, accrediting agencies. However, resources will be required to support the trainers' work. To ensure the success of this effort, it is important to develop a feasible strategy before embarking on the training process. Many PSIC graduates expressed interest in becoming a trainer by participating in the PSIC train-the-trainer program. They also identified the resources they would need to meaningfully assume the role of a trainer, including outside funding for time, travel, and teaching supplies; educational materials from the VA and AHRQ; reduced work responsibilities; support staff to handle administrative details; and a refresher course. In addition, trainees have noted that they need to have access to off-the-shelf tools that can be put to work readily in their training activities. The AHRQ/VA partnership is already well aware of many of these needs, and has plans to address them in the upcoming train-the-trainer program. We note these suggestions here merely as emphasis, given that many trainees specifically mentioned them.

- **Evaluate the suggestions of trainees on PSIC course structure and content for use in implementation of future PSIC training activities.** Trainees offered many suggestions about how to improve the current structure and content of the PSIC. While making all suggested changes is not likely to be feasible or, in some cases, desirable, AHRQ should consider the following key suggestions from the trainees:

  o Allow more time for networking—a component that trainees say is as important to them as the more traditional types of tools.

  o Ensure that each speaker knows the content of other teachers' lectures, in order to avoid repetition or overlap.

  o Invite past PSIC graduates to future training to serve on a panel regarding how they continued their projects, their experiences some years down the road, and what they wished they had done while attending the program. We note that the AHRQ/VA partnership foresaw the value of doing this and had already planned to ask past graduates to participate in future training prior to receiving suggestions from the trainees to do so. In including this suggestion here, we simply are emphasizing the interest expressed by trainees.

  o Provide assistance to trainees very early on in the program in selecting and developing a realistic plan to execute their project topic, helping them get a head start. As part of this assistance, PSIC teachers should encourage teams to get buy-in from their organizations early on so the project has the best chance of success and of continuing after training ends.

  o Provide more information on the following topics: reporting systems, patient safety in long-term care/nursing homes, the business case for patient safety/ROI, and examples of successful interventions and positive corrective actions.

- Provide more direction to hospitals regarding how to get physicians and the administrative/operational leadership to work together. Trainees sense continued tension in this regard but are not sure how to resolve it.

- Spread out patient safety–related conferences and workshops. Trainees found that there were too many AHRQ-sponsored events back to back, making attendance at several of them difficult, given the inability to be out of the office for weeks on end.

- Offer a specialized course for individuals who already know the basics of patient safety and would like to attend a patient safety course geared to a more sophisticated audience.

Appendix A
First Year 2003–2004 Team Interview Protocol

I. BACKGROUND INFORMATION

State Team:
Name(s) of team members:
Titles:
Interviewer:
Interview Date & Time:
RAND ID #:

II. CONSENT

Purpose of interview: RAND is conducting a multiyear evaluation of the Agency for Healthcare Research and Quality (AHRQ) patient safety initiative. As one part of our evaluation, we are examining the Patient Safety Improvement Corps (PSIC) program and the patient safety efforts of those who participated in the training.
Step 1: Read interviewees consent language. Ask all interviewees if they agree to be interviewed (this is their consent if they say yes).
Step 2: Ask if they have any questions before you get started.

III. INTERVIEW QUESTIONS

A. General Information on PSIC Participants

1. What is your role in your state/hospital/quality improvement organization (QIO)?

2. What led you to become involved in the PSIC?

3. What were your expectations about what you would learn or accomplish through your participation in the PSIC? (Were these expectations met?)

4. What did you understand to be the expectations of the training sponsors—AHRQ and the VA—in terms of your team's participation in the PSIC?

5. Has your original team configuration changed since the start of the PS Improvement Corps training? **If YES→** describe how it has changed and why changes were made. **If NO→** is that because they got good guidance from VA and AHRQ about how to configure their teams from the start and/or it very clear to them from the outset what they'd be doing vis-à-vis their participation (meaning the demands were clear and they could commit to doing the work required)?

B. Prior Knowledge/Experience of Participants

1. What was your level of knowledge about medical error, patient safety, and the risks and hazards in the system leading to patient injury due to the delivery of health care prior to your participation in the PSIC?

2. What was your level of familiarity with the tools used to investigate near misses, medical errors, and patient harm/injury resulting from the delivery of health care prior to your participation in the PSIC?

3. What was your level of experience in developing interventions to improve patient safety or reduce/mitigate the impact of medical errors prior to your participation in the PSIC?

4. What was your level of experience performing evaluations to assess the impact of programs or interventions designed to improve patient safety and reduce the opportunity for medical errors and their impact?

5. Did your state have a medical error reporting system when you started the PSIC training?

    a. If yes, please describe the system (what type of information it tracks, who submits, how data from system is shared with those who provide information).

        • Did you/have you used this system and how? (Or who uses this system and for what purposes?)
        • Has the system been altered as a result of your participation in the PSIC training? If not, does the PSIC training impact your plan to change the reporting system?

C. Content of PSIC training

1. Was the information provided during the training and in "homework assignments" targeted at the appropriate level for your experience and expertise going into the training? What challenges did you face in doing the work? (Get them to speak about specific assignments: the project, Root Cause Analysis, reading).

2. Have you used any of the training you've received thus far back in your current job? If yes, please describe what you've used and how you've applied it?

3. Have you engaged other folks that you work with to understand or learn the training techniques that you've been taught during the PSIC training?

4. What aspects of your training do you feel will prove most valuable to you in the future?

5. As a result of the PSIC training, do you feel you have the skills to (**YES/NO**)

   a. Select the appropriate tool to investigate an error or near miss?

   b. Conduct an investigation of a medical error or near miss and prepare reports based on your findings?

   c. Develop an intervention based on the findings from your investigation?

   d. Measure and evaluate the impact of the safety intervention you developed?

   e. Translate patient safety interventions into standard clinical practice?

6. Have you found group discussion of the case studies to be a valuable part of your training? **If yes**, why? **If no**, why not?

7. Were there particular topics not covered in the training that you feel should have been? If yes, please describe.

8. In your opinion, do you think the content of the training could be improved, and if yes, how?

9. Do you feel that you've been successful in completing the project that you selected for the PSIC? (**If yes**, why do you feel you were successful? **If no**, why not?)

10. What barriers, if any, did you face in conducting your project? How did you overcome them? (**Probe:** Were your CEOs involved and supportive to enable/facilitate you conducting your projects?)

D. Using the PSIC training

(NOTE: WE'RE PRIMARILY EVALUATING PSIC, BUT ALSO SEEK FEEDBACK ON THE VA TOOLS)

1. (FIND OUT FROM VA WHICH TEAMS HAVE DONE THIS), then start question—We understand you have used RCS or HFMEA. Have you conducted a root cause analysis (RCA) or Healthcare Failure Mode And Effect Analysis (HFMEA) since you started your training? **If YES**→were you able to identify contributing and underlying factors of the event? Have you used the forms included in your PSIC binders to aid in the performance of a RCA? Was this a valuable exercise?

2. What initiatives are you implementing or have you already implemented as a result of your patient safety training?

3. How would you assess your ability to continue to use these tools/methods/knowledge moving forward—in your future work? Do you think you'll continue to use them once the PSIC training has ended?

4. What do you feel or what have you found are the greatest barriers to implementing the tools, methods, knowledge, and information you have gained through the PSIC?

5. How helpful was the PSIC training in giving you skills or tools to make changes as part of your patient safety activities?

6. What resources would better facilitate your ability to use these patient safety methods, tools? Knowledge, information? Is there adequate support in your state/hospital for doing the kinds of things you learned through the PSIC training?

7. Have you used the materials included in your PSIC binders in your work activities? How valuable have you found them? Which have been the most useful to you?

8. How comfortable are you with the different types of data and methods that can be used to evaluate and monitor patient safety? Has the PSIC helped you to be able to use data better (either existing or different/better data)?

9. Have you undertaken efforts to systematically assess the safety culture in hospitals around your state? **If YES→**How would you describe the safety culture in hospitals around your state? Can you describe the type and the extent of variation that you've seen in what hospitals are doing about the patient safety culture? **If NO→**What might you do in the future to assess the patient safety culture in hospitals within your state?

10. Thinking ahead to the future, what type of initiatives could you envision being developed and implemented to improve the patient safety culture in hospitals around your state?

E. Concluding Questions

1. Are there other individuals in your state who you think would benefit from being taught the skills you learned during the last year through your participation in the PSIC? **If YES→** who?

2. Is there anything else you would like to tell us or think we should know about your experience in the PSIC program?

Appendix B
First Year 2003–2004 Follow-up Telephone Interview Protocol

I. BACKGROUND INFORMATION (To be filled in by recruiter prior to interview)

1. RAND ID for state:
2. RAND ID for individual interviewee:
3. State:
4. Name of organization:
5. Type of organization (i.e., state health department, hospital, other):
6. Name of interviewee:
7. Title of interviewee:
8. Year of PSIC training:
   (NOTE: They will all be 2003-04/Year 1 this year, but we want to add this field now in anticipation of next year's interviews with year 2 trainees.)
9. Does the state have a state-wide reporting system?
   a. *If yes:* Is it voluntary, mandatory, or both?
10. Was/were today's interviewee(s) interviewed at the 3rd PSIC training session of Year 1 (i.e., May 2004 in Washington DC)? (yes/no)
    a. *If yes:* Name of RAND interviewer (i.e., Cheryl Damberg, Allen Freemont, or Melony Sorbero)
11. Does this state have a team participating in the 2nd year/2004-05 PSIC training? (yes/no)
12. RAND interviewer:
13. Date of interview:
14. Phone number to call for interview:
15. Email of interviewee:

II. INFORMED CONSENT (responsibility of interviewer)

Note start time of interview.

Thank you for agreeing to speak with me today about your involvement in the AHRQ Patient Safety Improvement Corps (PSIC). Before we get started with the interview, I'd like to make sure you received our important introductory information.
Did you receive the letter and fact sheet that confirm our appointment today, describe our procedures, and explain this research study?

1. If yes received letter and fact sheet,

    a. Do you have any questions about the study?
       • *If yes questions, review this checklist:*

<u>Nature of the project and funder</u>
AHRQ has contracted with the RAND Corporation, a non-profit research institution headquartered in Santa Monica, California, to serve as the Evaluation Center for the national patient safety program operated by AHRQ in collaboration with other federal agencies.

In order to advance knowledge and implement patient safety improvements, RAND is charged with examining the history and current status of the patient safety program, and with assessing the activities of AHRQ and its funded grantees

<u>Why they were selected to participate and what we will be asking</u>
We are interested in speaking to you because you have participated in the PSIC training program, the partnership program of AHRQ and the VA to improve patient safety. We would like to learn about your experiences as a PSIC trainee.

We are particularly interested to find out how your participation in the PSIC training program has impacted your organization's efforts to improve patient safety as well as your thoughts about how the PSIC may be improved.

<u>The information collected is for research purposes only</u>
We will not release information that identifies you to anyone outside the research team, except as required by law.

We will destroy all information that identifies you at the end of the study.

<u>Respondent rights</u>
You do not have to participate in this interview, and we can stop at any time for any reason.

Your participation or nonparticipation will not be reported to anyone.

Please feel free to decline to discuss any topic that we raise.

If no questions, proceed to b.

    b. Do you agree to participate in our research interview?

2. If no, did not receive letter and fact sheet,

    a. Read the following to the respondent:
    The Agency for Healthcare Research and Quality (AHRQ) has contracted with the RAND Corporation, a non-profit research institution headquartered in Santa Monica, California, to serve as the Evaluation Center for the national patient safety program operated by AHRQ in collaboration with other federal agencies. In a four-year evaluation, RAND is charged with examining the history and current status of the patient safety program and assessing the activities of the Agency and its funded grantees to

advance knowledge and implement patient safety improvements. As part of this effort, RAND is evaluating the Patient Safety Improvement Corps (PSIC), the partnership program of AHRQ and Department of Veterans Affairs (VA) to improve patient safety.

We are interested in speaking to you because you have participated in the PSIC training program. We would like to learn about your experiences as a PSIC trainee. We are particularly interested to find out how your participation in the PSIC training program has impacted your organization's efforts to improve patient safety as well as your thoughts about how the PSIC may be improved.

RAND will use the information you provide for research purposes only, and will not disclose your identity or information that identifies you to anyone outside of the research project, except as required by law. We will destroy all information that identifies you at the end of the study.

You do not have to participate in the interview, and we can stop at any time for any reason. Your participation or nonparticipation will not be reported to anyone. You should feel free to decline to discuss any topic that we raise.

b. Do you have any questions about the study?

c. Do you agree to participate in our research interview?

3. Whom to Contact about this Research (if respondent inquires)
Donna O. Farley, Ph.D.
RAND
201 N. Craig Street
Pittsburgh, PA 15213
Telephone: 412-683-2300
FAX: 412-683-2800
Email: Donna_Farley@rand.org

Tora K. Bikson, Ph.D.
RAND
1776 Main Street, P.O. Box 2138
Santa Monica CA 90407-2138
Telephone: 310-393-0411
FAX: 310-393-4818
Email: Tora_Bikson@rand.org

III. INTERVIEW QUESTIONS

Ok. Let's get started! Last year, RAND—under contract from AHRQ—interviewed many of the trainees participating in this program. We are now conducting follow-up interviews with all 2003-04 trainees to understand whether and how you have been able to use the PSIC skills and tools, and whether you have encountered any challenges in the process.

A. Introduction/Ice-breaker

1. If we talked to this individual and/or team last year at the 3rd training session in Washington DC, acknowledge that fact.

2. Describe the given state's project as we understand it from: 1) the power point presentation given at the 3rd training session, and 2) from the notes from our Washington DC interview, if this team was interviewed by us last year/we have notes from last year's DC interview.

> *a. Confirm that our understanding of the project is accurate/ note clarifications.*

> *b. If we did NOT interview this individual/team last year OR do not have notes from last year's DC interview:* Please briefly tell me a little about your team (e.g., how it was formed, the different roles of team members, etc.).
> - *Probe*: Please describe your job responsibilities.

B. Attendance and Support Needed to Attend PSIC Training

First, I'd like to ask you a few questions about your attendance at the PSIC training and the support needed to be part of the training.

1. How many training sessions did you attend?

Check the box next to the number of training sessions attended	
1	☐
2	☐
3	☐

2. Please describe the type of support or arrangements that your organization made in order for you to attend the PSIC training and to complete the assignments you were given?

3. Do you feel that you were you given adequate support to fully participate in the PSIC training and complete your team's project?
- *Probes*: Adequate time, staff to cover your duties while you were out?

4. Were there any barriers that you had to overcome in order to attend or to fully engage in the training?
> *If yes:* Please describe.

5. Were there any changes in the configuration of your team's membership over the course of the PSIC training?

    If yes: What changes were made and why? Please explain.

6. What would you tell organizations that might be interested in sending staff to the PSIC training about the level of support from their own organizations that they realistically should expect to provide?

C. Usefulness of PSIC Tools/Skills and Help Needed

Next, I'd like to learn about how useful you found the skills and tools taught at the PSIC training.

1. What aspects of the PSIC training were most valuable to you?

    a. Why?

2. As evaluators of AHRQ's patient safety activities, our goal is to document the usefulness of the different aspects of the PSIC training. In the following section of the interview, I would like to go through a list of about a dozen key tools/skills taught through the PSIC training and ask you some questions about the usefulness of each one to you and your organization. This section is the most tedious part of the interview so please bear with me as we go through this list!

Tool/Skills	Useful overall? (yes/no/don't know)	Why or why not?	Actually use in practice? (yes/no/don't know)	If yes, how? If no, why not?
Error Analysis				
a. Root Cause Analysis (RCA)				
b. Failure Mode and Effect Analysis (HFMEA)				
c. Probabilistic Risk Assessment (PRA)				
d. VA's Safety Assessment Code (SAC)				
Human Factors				
e. Human Factors Engineering				
Safety Culture				
f. Patient safety culture survey/tools				
Monitoring				
g. Patient safety indicators (PSIs)				
h. Tools to identify high-alert medications				
i. Analysis of patient safety data				

Tool/Skills	Useful overall? (yes/no/don't know)	Why or why not?	Actually use in practice? (yes/no/don't know)	If yes, how? If no, why not?
Reporting				
j. Reporting of Adverse Events/Near Misses				
Other				
k. Tools to assess the business case for patient safety				
l. Tools to evaluate patient safety programs				
m. Other; describe:				

3. Regarding the skills and/or tools taught through the PSIC training that you do not currently use in practice <u>but would like to</u>, what would help you use them?

    a. After completion of the training, would technical support or assistance from AHRQ or the VA be useful to you on an on-going basis?
- *If interviewee asks, examples of technical support include but are not limited to things like a telephone help line to call with questions about how or when to use a certain tool, what sample size is needed for a given analysis, etc, etc.*

    b. *If yes:* Please describe what specifically would be helpful to you.

4. In general, in instances when you felt that you needed help or guidance to use the tools or apply the skills you learned through the PSIC training, what sorts of resources (if any) have you been able to draw on since the PSIC training?
- *Probe: If got help,* From where? Other PSIC team members? Other states? Elsewhere?

    a. Do you think that on-going support from the VA, AHRQ, or some other entity would help you to maintain or enhance your skills or use tools effectively after the PSIC training?

5. Have you found the books and other resources you received as part of the PSIC training to be helpful post training? Please describe/explain.
- *Probe: Names/titles/descriptions of most useful resources.*

   a. Did you share these materials with others in your organization (i.e., those who did not attend the training)?

D. Impact of PSIC on Patient Safety Action(s)

I'd now like to ask you a few questions about the impact of the PSIC training on patient safety activities in your organization or state.

1. First, I'm going to go through a list of patient safety-related actions and would like you to tell me whether the PSIC training that you participated in contributed to or facilitated any of them. *Proceed to appropriate checklist below.*

   a. Checklist for state representatives: Please tell me whether the PSIC training that you participated in contributed to or facilitated any of the following:

Patient Safety Action for State Representatives	Yes	No
i. Initiation of or influence on regulation(s)/legislation ➢ Describe:	☐	☐
ii. Creation of a state-wide reporting system ➢ Describe: ➢ *Probe:* Mandatory, voluntary, or both?	☐	☐
iii. Modification of an existing state reporting system to improve how it captures patient safety issues or how information is reported to others ➢ Describe:	☐	☐
iv. Modification of hospital oversight procedures when an adverse event occurs (e.g., change content of Root Cause Analysis/RCA) ➢ Describe:	☐	☐
v. New membership in or formation of a patient safety coalition of stakeholders ➢ Describe:	☐	☐
vi. Other ➢ Describe:	☐	☐

b. Checklist for <u>hospitals and other organizations within the state</u>: Please tell me whether the PSIC training that you participated in contributed to or facilitated any of the following:

Patient Safety Action for Hospitals and Other Organizations Within the State	Yes	No
i. Creation of an institutional adverse event reporting system ➤ Describe:	☐	☐
ii. Modification of processes to review/analyze adverse events or errors ➤ Describe:	☐	☐
iii. Sharing data across organizations to better understand causes of error ➤ Describe:	☐	☐
iv. New membership in or formation of a patient safety group of stakeholders ➤ Describe:	☐	☐
v. Promotion of patient safety culture ➤ Describe:	☐	☐
vi. Other changes in review of adverse events ➤ Describe:	☐	☐
vii. Other state- wide or organization-wide initiatives ➤ Describe:	☐	☐

2. *If PSIC training helped to stimulate action, ask:*

   a. Why do you think this has happened?

   b. How influential was the PSIC training in bringing about these changes?

3. *If PSIC training did <u>not</u> help stimulate action, ask:*

   a. Why has no action occurred?
         • *Probe:* Any barriers?

E. Contact with PSIC-related Colleagues and Support Staff

The next set of questions has to do with your contact with other PSIC-related colleagues and staff.

1. Are you still in contact with any of the following?

Contact with:	Yes	No
a. Your PSIC team members (i.e., those from <u>your</u> state with whom you participated in the PSIC training)	☐	☐
b. Members of other PSIC teams (i.e., those from <u>other</u> states who participated in the PSIC training at the same time you did)	☐	☐
c. Staff from the VA	☐	☐
d. Staff from AHRQ	☐	☐

2. *For items checked "yes" above,* please describe the nature and frequency of your interactions.

F. Helpfulness of PSIC Training/Advice to Others

Next, I'd like to get a sense from you about how helpful you found the PSIC training.

1. On a scale of 1 to 10, with 1 being not at all helpful and 10 being very helpful, how valuable would you say the PSIC training has been in improving the process(es) you use to monitor and improve patient safety?

Not at all   **Very helpful**
helpful

1	2	3	4	5	6	7	8	9	10
☐	☐	☐	☐	☐	☐	☐	☐	☐	☐

    a. Which aspects of the PSIC training most influenced your rating?

    b. What, if anything, do you think you are doing better <u>on a day-to-day basis</u> as a direct result of your involvement in the PSIC training?
- *Probe if doing better:* What made it possible for you to improve? What would help you further improve?
- *Probes if <u>not</u> doing better:* What have been the barriers? What help could you use to overcome them?

2. On a scale of 1 to 10, with 1 being not recommend at all and 10 being recommend enthusiastically, what would you say <u>to a state</u> that is contemplating participation in a PSIC training program?

Not   **Recommend**
recommend   **enthusiastically**
at all

1	2	3	4	5	6	7	8	9	10
☐	☐	☐	☐	☐	☐	☐	☐	☐	☐

3. On a scale of 1 to 10, with 1 being not recommend at all and 10 being recommend enthusiastically, what would you say <u>to a hospital or other provider organization</u> that is contemplating participation in a PSIC training program?

Not   **Recommend**
recommend   **enthusiastically**
at all

1	2	3	4	5	6	7	8	9	10
☐	☐	☐	☐	☐	☐	☐	☐	☐	☐

4. If you had it to do over again, knowing what you know now, would you participate in the PSIC training? Why/why not?

5. What types of staff would you recommend that an organization send to the PSIC training?

G. Train-the-Trainer

Through the PSIC, AHRQ is making a significant investment in training individuals from all 50 states over a three-year period to have the skills and tools needed to improve patient safety in the "real world." In Year 4, AHRQ will shift the focus of the PSIC to a "train-the-trainer" model through which it will teach teams how to train others within their state about patient safety skills and tools. The hope is that these teams will expand the number of people across the United States who have the skills and tools to make safety improvements in a variety of practice settings.

1. Although it was not an expectation or requirement of the PSIC training sessions you participated in, have you been able to train others within your organization, community, and/or state about the tools and skills you learned through the PSIC training?

    a. If yes, How? Please describe.
- *Probe:* Would you be willing to send us a copy of your meeting agenda, slides, etc from the training you did?

    b. If no, Why not?

2. Would you be interested in serving as a trainer to others in your state?

    a. If yes, what kind of support/resources would you need to do this?

    b. If no, why not?
- *Probe:* Not enough resources? If a hospital, is interaction with competitors not encouraged?

H. "Refresher" Activity/Course

We're almost finished! Next, I'd like to get a sense of your interest in additional training.

1. If AHRQ were to offer additional PSIC training (i.e., some sort of "refresher" course or activity), would this be of interest to you?

    a. *If yes,* what would you want this activity to include/what would you want to learn? Please describe what would be most helpful to you.
- *Probe:* What type of support or time would you need to be able to participate in the refresher activity?

    b. *If no,* why not?

I.   Conclusion/Wrap up

We're at the end!

1. Do you have any other thoughts about the PSIC training that you would like to share or any suggestions?
- *Probe:* Is there anything else I did not ask you about that you would like to mention?

Thank you for your time. Your insights and feedback about the PSIC training program are important to us.

❖ *Note end time of interview:*

Appendix C
Second Year 2004–2005 Team Interview Protocol

I. BACKGROUND INFORMATION
1. State:
2. Information about each team member:

Name	Organization	Title	Individual RAND ID#	Participating in this interview? (Yes/No)

3. Does the state have a state-wide reporting system?
   a. *If yes:* Is it voluntary, mandatory, or both?
4. RAND Interviewer:
5. Interview Date:
6. RAND ID for state:

II. CONSENT

❖ *Note start time of interview.*

1. Introduce yourself.

2. Review the purpose of the interview:
   - RAND is conducting a multi-year evaluation of the Agency for Healthcare Research and Quality (AHRQ) patient safety initiative.
   - As one part of our evaluation, we are examining the Patient Safety Improvement Corps (PSIC) program and the patient safety efforts of those participating in the training.
   - We would like to learn about your experiences as a PSIC trainee.

3. Review informed consent:
   - The information collected is for research purposes only:
     o We will not release information that identifies you to anyone outside the research team, except as required by law.
     o We will destroy all information that identifies you at the end of the study.
   - You have the following rights as a respondent:
     o You do not have to participate in this interview.
     o We can stop at any time for any reason.
     o Your participation or nonparticipation will not be reported to anyone.
     o You may decline to discuss any topic that we raise.

4. Do you agree to be interviewed?

5. Do you have any questions before we get started?

III. FOCUS GROUP QUESTIONS

A. General Information on PSIC Participants

1. What role do you play in your state, hospital, or quality improvement organization (QIO)?
    - *Probe:* What are your job responsibilities?

2. What led your organization to become involved in the PSIC?

3. What were your expectations about what you would learn or accomplish through your participation in the PSIC?

4. What did you understand to be the expectations of AHRQ and the VA in terms of your team's participation in the PSIC?

5. Has your original team configuration changed since the start of the PSIC training?
    - *If yes:* How has it changed? Why were these changes made?

B. Prior Knowledge/Experience of Participants

1. With 1 being no experience/expertise at all and 5 being very experienced/having a high level of expertise, please tell me what your level of experience or expertise was in the following areas prior to your participation in the PSIC.

> NOTE: If answers differ for each team member, write name of each in cell corresponding to rating.

Area	1	2	3	4	5
	No experience/ expertise at all				High level of experience/ expertise
a. Medical error, patient safety, and the risks and hazards in the system leading to patient injury due to the delivery of health care.					
b. Tools used to investigate near misses, medical errors, and patient harm/injury resulting from the delivery of health care.					
c. Interventions to improve patient safety or reduce/mitigate the impact of medical errors.					
d. Evaluation techniques to assess the impact of programs, or interventions designed to improve patient safety and reduce the opportunity for medical errors and their impact.					

2. State Reporting Systems

   a. *If state has reporting system, ask:*
   - Please describe your reporting system (i.e., what type of information it tracks, who submits the information, and how data from the system are shared with those who provide information).
   - Have you used this system and how (i.e., for what purpose(s))?
   - How useful have you found the system?
   - Through the PSIC training, have you learned anything that would make you want to alter your current system?
       - *If yes,* please describe any changes and whether you could see yourself involved in helping to bring about these changes.
       - *Probe:* Has your system actually been altered as a function of your involvement in the PSIC?

   b. *If state does not have reporting system, ask:*

- Based on what you have learned through your participation in the PSIC, do you anticipate working to implement a reporting system in the future?
- Why/why not?

C. Content of PSIC Training and Interaction Among Teams

1. Was the information provided during the training and in homework/reading assignments targeted at the appropriate level for your experience and expertise going into the training?
   - *Probe:* What challenges did you face in doing the work? What tasks, readings, or assignments were particularly challenging?

2. Thus far, have you used any of the skills/tools of the PSIC training in your current job?
   - *If yes,* please describe what you have used and how you have applied it?
   - *If no,* have there been any barriers? Please explain.

3. Have you introduced any of the PSIC skills/tools that you have been taught to any of your colleagues in your home state?

4. What aspects of your training do you feel will prove most valuable to you in the future?

5. With 1 being not at all skilled and 5 being very skilled, please tell me what your skill level is in the following areas, <u>as a result of the PSIC training</u>.

NOTE: If answers differ for each team member, write name of each in cell corresponding to rating.

Area	1 Not at all skilled	2	3	4	5 Very skilled
a. Select the appropriate tool(s) to investigate an error or near miss.					
b. Conduct an investigation of a medical error or near miss and prepare reports based on your findings.					
c. Develop an intervention based on the findings from your investigation.					
d. Measure and evaluate the impact of the safety intervention you developed.					
e. Translate patient safety interventions into standard clinical practice.					

6. Have you participated in any of the VA's optional telephone meetings to discuss your projects?

    a. *If yes*, have you found them to be helpful? Why/why not?

    b. *If no,* why not?

    c. What recommendations do you have for the VA to help make these telephone meetings more useful for you?

7. Have you had any other interactions that have been helpful to you as you have worked on your team project?
   - *Probes*: Email contact with AHRQ or VA? In-person conversations with other states at first two training sessions? Individual phone calls/emails with other states between training sessions?

8. Were there particular topics not covered in the training that you feel should have been included? How do you think the content of the training could be improved?
   - *Probe for details.*

9. Do you feel that you have been successful in completing the project that you selected for the PSIC?
   - *Probe:* Why/why not?

10. What barriers, if any, did you face in conducting your project? How did you overcome them?
    - *Probe:* Were your CEOs involved in and supportive of your involvement in your PSIC project? Did they provide the help you needed to conduct your project?

D. Using the PSIC training

1. I am aware of your general project topic. Can you please tell me a little more about which PSIC tools and skills you used to carry out your project?
   - *Probe:* Did you conduct a Root Cause Analysis (RCA), Health care Failure Mode And Effect Analysis (HFMEA), or use a culture survey? If yes, how did it go? Any problems? What did you learn?

2. Have you implemented or are you currently implementing any initiatives as a result of your patient safety training?
   - *If yes,* please describe.
   - *If no,* have there been any barriers?

3. Do you think you will use the PSIC tools/skills once the training has ended?
   - *Probe:* Why/why not?

4. What have you found to be the greatest barriers to implementing the skills and tools you have learned through the PSIC?

5. Have you used the materials provided to you during the PSIC training in your day-to-day work activities?

- *Probe:* Why/why not?
- *Probe if use them:* How valuable have you found them? Which have been the most useful to you?

6. How comfortable are you with the different types of data and methods that can be used to evaluate and monitor patient safety?
    - *Probe:* Has the PSIC helped you be able to use data better (either existing or different/better data)?

7. Recently (i.e., in the last 1-2 years), have you undertaken efforts to systematically assess the safety culture in hospitals around your state?

- *Probe if yes:*
    - Please describe the tool(s) you used.
    - How would you describe the safety culture in hospitals around your state?
    - Please describe the type and the extent of variation that you have seen in what hospitals are doing about patient safety culture?
    - In the future, what types of initiatives could you envision being developed and implemented to improve the patient safety culture in hospitals within your state?

- *Probe if no:*
    - In the future, what types of initiatives could you envision being developed and implemented to improve the patient safety culture in hospitals within your state?
    - What might you be willing/able to do to help in this effort?

E. Concluding Questions

1. Are there other individuals in your state whom you think would benefit from participating in the PSIC?
    - *If yes, obtain names and contact information if possible.*

2. Is there anything else you would like to tell us or think we should know about your experience in the PSIC program?

References

Agency for Healthcare Research and Quality (AHRQ), Patient Safety Network Glossary: http://www.psnet.ahrq.gov/glossary.aspx, 2006

———, "Patient Safety Improvement Corps: An AHRQ/VA Partnership," (Fact Sheet): http://www.ahrq.gov/about/psimpcorps.htm, 2006

Bridge Medical, Inc., *Beyond Blame* (video). Solana Beach, CA. (Distributed through the Institute for Safe Medication Practices [ISMP]), 1988.

DeRosier, J., Stalhandske, E., Bagian, J.P., and Nudell, T. "Using health care Failure Mode and Effect Analysis: the VA National Center for Patient Safety's Prospective Risk Analysis System." *Joint Commission Journal on Quality Improvement.* Vol. 28(5): 248-67, 2002, 209.

Institute for Safe Medication Practices: http://www.ismp.org/Tools/highalertmedications.pdf, 2006

Institute of Medicine (IOM), *To Err Is Human: Building a Safer Health System.* L. T. Kohn, J. M. Corrigan, and M. S. Donaldson, eds., Washington, D.C.: National Academy Press, 2000.

———, *Crossing the Quality Chasm: A New Health System for the 21st Century.* Committee on Quality of Health Care in America, Washington, D.C.: National Academy Press, 2002.

Joint Commission on Accreditation of Healthcare Organizations (JCAHO): http://www.jointcommission.org/SentinelEvents/, 2006.

Kizer, K.W. and Stegun, M.B. "Serious Reportable Adverse Events in Health Care" in *Advances in Patient Safety*, Vol. 4; 339-352, 2005.

Marx, D. "Probabilistic Risk Assessment," Presentation at PSIC Training, Washington, D.C., 2005.

McDonald, K., P. Romans, J. Geppert, et al., *Measures of Patient Safety Based on Hospital Administrative Data—the Patient Safety Indicators*, Rockville, MD.: AHRQ, Publication No. 02-0038, 2002.

National Quality Forum (NQF), *Serious Reportable Events in Healthcare: A Consensus Report*, Washington, D.C., 2003.

Norman, Donald A. *The Design of Everyday Things.* New York: Doubleday, 1990.

Quality Interagency Coordination Task Force (QuIC). *Doing What Counts for Patient Safety: Federal Actions to Reduce Medical Errors and Their Impact*, Rockville, MD., 2000.

Reason, James T. *Managing the Risks of Organizational Accidents.* Ashgate, VT: Aldershot, Hants, England and Brookfield, 1997.

U.S. Department of Veterans Affairs National Center for Patient Safety, Personal communication with Stephanie Teleki, 2006.

Veterans Health Administration (VHA). *The VHA National Patient Safety Improvement Handbook* (VHA Handbook 1050.1), Washington, D.C.: VHA, 2002.

Weick, Karl E. and Sutcliffe, Kathleen M. *Managing the Unexpected: Assuring High Performance in an Age of Complexity.* San Francisco: Jossey-Bass, 2001